POLITIC SHOCK

Praise for the book

History, predicted Francis Fukuyama in 1989, would end with the triumph of liberal democracy. In this superb panoramic survey of world politics and economics, Meghnad Desai explains how and why history has resumed its sway. Introducing a fascinating comparison between Donald Trump and Indian Prime Minister Narendra Modi, Desai expertly navigates the challenges to the Western-based liberal order of Islamic fundamentalism, the rise of Asia, economic stagnation, the new digital technology and populism. The future, he concludes, is uncertain, but Desai's faith in human decency shines through.

—**Lord Robert Skidelsky**,
Emeritus Professor of Political Economy,
University of Warwick

A masterpiece from the master of geopolitics. Meghnad Desai puts the rise of Modi and Trump into long-running historical context and draws conclusions that are relevant for everyone interested in the future of political leadership across our planet.

—**David Marsh**,
Managing Director and Co-Founder,
Official Monetary and Financial Institutions Forum

The curiosity and anxiety about populism—and the way it has moved centre stage in world politics to subvert the liberal order—have spawned some delightful recent books. Now, Meghnad Desai has done what was waiting to be done. *Politicshock* is his wry, ambivalent panegyric to the liberal order which, in alliance with the ruling culture of the global political economy, claims the right to redefine the current topography of democracy. This is an excellent, highly readable account of the changing profile of the triad. Here, to disappoint you, there are no heroes and no villains, unless you identify shortsighted political realism and gullible, media-struck, infantilized citizens as invisible actors in human affairs.

—**Ashis Nandy**
Honorary Fellow,
Centre for the Study of Developing Societies

POLITIC SHOCK

Trump, Modi, Brexit & the Prospect for Liberal Democracy

MEGHNAD DESAI

RUPA

Published by
Rupa Publications India Pvt. Ltd 2017
7/16, Ansari Road, Daryaganj
New Delhi 110002

Sales Centres:
Allahabad Bengaluru Chennai
Hyderabad Jaipur Kathmandu
Kolkata Mumbai

Copyright © Meghnad Desai 2017

The views and opinions expressed in this book are the author's own and the facts are as reported by him which have been verified to the extent possible, and the publishers are not in any way liable for the same.

All rights reserved.

No part of this publication may be reproduced, transmitted, or stored in a retrieval system, in any form or by any means, electronic, mechanical, photocopying, recording or otherwise, without the prior permission of the publisher.

ISBN: 978-81-291-4839-1

First impression 2017

10 9 8 7 6 5 4 3 2 1

The moral right of the author has been asserted.

Printed in India by Replika Press Pvt. Ltd.

This book is sold subject to the condition that it shall not, by way of trade or otherwise, be lent, resold, hired out, or otherwise circulated, without the publisher's prior consent, in any form of binding or cover other than that in which it is published.

For
Padam and Rajini Rosha
with respect and affection

ALL I CAN THINK OF IS YOU

By Sven Desai

I wanted to write a piece about
How free movement of capital
Allows the evasion of national regulations
And political control
Piling up mile high-guarded mountains of gold
But all I can think of is you.

I wanted to write a piece about
How the value of networks being a function of their size
Combines with the weightless economy
And digital goods to facilitate global monopolies
That bleeds the world dry
Feeding small pools of leeches
In Seattle offices
But all I can think of is the time
You wore Gothic eye makeup with silver studs.

I wanted to write about
How all-encompassing property rights
Within a system of profit incentives encourage
Rent extraction of our common heritage
Co-opting distributed pillage
Like a virus defiling the planet
But my mind is filled with the image
Of you in a white bonnet with flowers and beau lace
And all I can think of is you.

I wanted to write
A polemic about how the efficacy and endemic limits
Of bureaucratic administration creates a situation
Where the government is buckling under its own weight.
How the width at the base determines
A pyramid's safe height
But my mind
Keeps going back to that fight we had on the stairs.

I wanted to write about
How surpassed nationalism is floundering
Due to the decimation of capital cost of broadcast.
The geography of communication fields bequeathed
By Mongolian, North Atlantic and Islamic imperialism
In comparison to our border being a hundred miles
But all I can think of is
You brushing your hair
From your smile, compassionate, confused.

I wanted to write about intellectual property

As a simple conceptual heresy against
The inherent advantages of humanity, GNU
The defence of academy to protect
The intellectual future of our race as the task
Of the present generation to gift.

About the necessity of using our freedom
To develop new institutions, forms of cooperation
Demonstrative architectures of distribution
And possible uses of block-chain for value inclusion.
I wanted to write about a new Rochdale
But I fail
Cos my mind is locked on the picture
Of coloured string in your pigtails
And all I can think of is you.

I wanted to write about
Transnational communication, the evolution
And creation of new communal identities
The necessary inabilities of global hierarchy
Against mathematically proven efficiency
And resilience of networks meaning
Their dominance is given
And consequent logical implications for feminism.
But all I can think of is your spinning hem
And feet,
A second of silence after when our eyes meet
And your whites, wide, just for moment
Tell me.
All I can think of is you.

CONTENTS

Preface / xiii

1. 2016: The Year the Old Order Collapsed / 1

2. Outsiders in Politics: Narendra Modi and Donald Trump / 66

3. Modi and Trump at Work / 88

4. Economics and Politics of Nationalism / 109

5. The Resurgence of Asia / 139

6. Quo Vadis? / 165

Postscript / 180

Acronyms / 183

Index / 197

PREFACE

This book began as an attempt to write an outline of the history of how we came to be in the present state of the world before Brexit or Trump. Chapter 1 is built around that theme. However, Brexit in June 2016 and Trump's election in November 2016 inspired a much larger debate among writers and political leaders about the discontent revealed in the two votes. I had been tracking the election campaign of Trump and have compared him to Narendra Modi whose success, like Trump's, was unpredicted and was largely unwelcome when it happened. I see them both as outsiders to their political establishments who have by their success shaken up the complacency of the old order. This forms the crux of Chapters 2 and 3.

The book also discusses the issues of populism and nationalism which now are cast as 'undesirable' tendencies. It is presumptuous, in my view, to cast either as an unmitigated 'bad'. I explore the economics and politics of nationalism in Chapter 4. Asia has emerged as a new and dynamic presence in the last hundred years, and I trace its unique achievements as a challenge to the Western Liberal Order. China could very well be the super power of this century. In that lie some dangers as well as opportunities for India, as highlighted in Chapter 5. The last chapter is a speculation on future trends which have already cast their shadows and could transform our lives.

I am grateful to David Marsh and Robert Skidelsky for having read the book in the draft form and improving it.

I thank Sven Desai for letting me reproduce his poem.

ONE

2016: THE YEAR THE OLD ORDER COLLAPSED

There are dates in history which are iconic because of events which took place on those dates, whose impact has been felt by many countries beyond the border of where they occurred and beyond the dates when they did. Just to take the Western examples. There is the year 1688 which marked the English Bloodless Revolution, the year 1776, the American Declaration of Independence, then 1789, the fall of Bastille and the start of the French Revolution, the year 1815, the Battle of Waterloo and the defeat of Napoleon, the year 1848 which saw the widespread uprising in favour of democracy across Western Europe and in the twentieth century 1914, 1917, 1939, 1945 and many more.

Will the year 2016 be similarly marked in history as the year when there was a dramatic political shift across the world? When the Old Order—the Liberal Order (LO hereafter), which had set the agenda over the previous fifty years—had a number of reverses? Just take a few instances of what has happened so far. In Brazil, Dilma Rousseff, the first woman president and a socialist, was impeached for corruption and had to resign. The former president of South Korea, Park Geun-hye, another woman to be the first president of her country, faced impeachment. The Philippines elected Rodrigo Duterte as president and he has promised to shoot drug dealers dead without recourse to law as well as denounced the American concern about human rights. In the United Kingdom (UK), in a referendum where 72 per cent of the electorate took part (much higher than in general elections), the majority voted to leave the European Union (EU), which the UK had joined in 1972. This sent a shock wave through the political system, which is coming to terms with what is being described as a 'populist' revolt against the elite.* There are charges of racism and xenophobia against the winning majority. In Italy, the voters rejected a proposal for constitutional reform advanced by former Prime Minister Matteo Renzi, which led to his resignation. The country faced a banking crisis at the time but that did not impress voters. There are parties across continental Europe which have broken the two-party political set-up—in Greece, Spain, Italy, the Netherlands, Germany and France. Parties of the extreme left and right have made their mark. An anti-Muslim party, Partij voor de Vrijheid (Party for Freedom or PVV) led by Geert Wilders,

---

*The word 'populist' was not always a term of denigration. Nineteenth-century America, where the word and the movement it characterizes originate, regarded it as a respectable attempt by farmers to take on the moneyed power of industrialists and robber barons.

has gained popularity in the Netherlands. In France, the presidential elections during April and May 2017 showed the collapse of the two established parties of the left and right. An outsider with impeccable liberal credentials, Emmanuel Macron, defeated another outsider of the extreme right, Marine Le Pen. While the liberal world was relieved, the collapse of the middle and the victory of an outsider are portents of future trouble.

The real big shock of 2016 was without doubt the election of Donald Trump against all expectations and predictions by almost all polls. Once again the liberal elite was shocked and in denial that its candidate Hillary Clinton could be displaced by someone who broke all rules of polite behaviour and speech. There are fears of a revival of white nationalism, racism and xenophobia against Muslims and Mexicans.

New Statesman, a veteran of the British Social Democratic Left, wrote in editorial in its issue of November (2016):

> The United States, the most powerful nation on Earth, will soon be led by an unashamed racist, misogynist and authoritarian. Mr Trump admires the Russian president, Vladimir Putin, whose rule is the greatest threat to Europe's security, and denies the reality of anthropogenic climate change, the greatest threat to our planet's future. The belligerence of the president-elect's 'America First' rhetoric should not be mistaken for incoherence. Mr Trump will disregard human rights at home and abroad in pursuit of whatever he thinks is the best option, at any given time.*

**New Statesman*. 2016. 'Leader: Trump and the Liberal Order', *New Statesman*, 17 November.

What is the breach which has been made? What is the LO which has been challenged? Is this an enduring shift or just a temporary aberration? If the LO was to be defeated, what will take its place? How soon will the New Order establish its hegemony, and how long would it last?

What is/was the LO?

The LO has been taken for granted as the ruling hegemony of ideas and attitudes and sees itself as liberal and tolerant, against racial, gender and all other forms of discrimination. It has a universal, cosmopolitan view of citizenship. It favours market economy and free trade across the world, subject to prudent regulation of markets. It believes that globalization has delivered peace and prosperity, though there are worries about the recent rise of inequality. Political leaders, academics, the print and visual media, arts and entertainment industry, the financial world—all are part of the LO. It is global, friendly and confident of its hegemony over culture, opinion and actions. It has been like this for the last fifty years, since the ushering in of John F. Kennedy as the president of the United States of America (USA).

A Century Ago

One could tell the history of the LO in a series of overlapping phases. A convenient starting point is a hundred years ago when two events occurred which shaped the twentieth century: the entry of America into the First World War in 1917 and a turbulent revolt in Russia against the czar in February which climaxed as the Bolshevik

Revolution (8 March–7 November 1917). The era of the nineteenth-century Concert of Europe, set up at the Congress of Vienna after the 1815 Battle of Waterloo, was over. European domination was waning. A century of Pax Britannica, which had helped Great Britain run a global empire and be the hegemonic military and economic power, was coming to an end.

After the end of the First World War in 1918, there was a twenty-year period when the world went through the Great Depression, the rise of fascism in Italy and Spain and, in a more virulent form, of Nazism in Germany. Russia dropped out of the capitalist system and survived years of blockade, civil war and famines to emerge as a formidable power as the Union of Soviet Socialist Republics (USSR), or just the Soviet Union.

The capitalist system, which had delivered steady growth through the nineteenth century (albeit helping the European imperial powers prosper more than the rest), fell into one of its deeper crises. The Bank of England could no longer manage the global financial system as it had been doing. But no one else was ready. America's Federal Reserve System, its central bank, was not even two full decades old when the crisis struck, and lacked the experience to be able to manage it. The world economy faltered. Banks failed in Europe and across America. The Great Depression, which began with a Wall Street crash in 1929, plunged all liberal capitalist economies into a decade and more of high and persistent unemployment. In contrast, the fascist economies managed to maintain full employment by ignoring the rules of orthodox finance and building up their armaments. The Soviet Union launched its planned economy, showing how full employment and steady growth could be achieved. There was no doubt that the leadership of the global order was in dispute.

A World of Cold War

The Second World War settled one issue—the leadership of the LO passed from Europe to USA.

As they lost their leadership, European imperial powers started confronting rebellion in their colonies. Over the next fifty years, one theme which emerged was the decolonization of Africa, Asia and the Caribbean. For Great Britain, the biggest imperial power, starting from the independence of India in 1947 to the handover of Hong Kong to China in 1997, marked the story of the end of the empire 'upon which the sun never set'. Europe's domination of Asia, what one historian called the 'Vasco Da Gama Era', inaugurated in 1498, ended five hundred years later.*

Western Europe lost the leadership of the global order. But who won? The next fifty years from 1945 to 1995 were to settle that issue. The Allies—USA, Great Britain, USSR (including France, which had surrendered to Germany and China which had fought Japan)—joined hands to defeat Germany and Japan. They set up the United Nations (UN) with the five Allies as permanent members of the Security Council with veto powers. But it was clear that among the five, some were more equal than others. USA and USSR were the two dominant powers that drew a line across Europe to define their 'spheres of influence'. USSR got Eastern Europe and west of the Elbe was the US sphere.

The peace and friendship among the Allies did not last. America had the atom bomb, which it used twice on Japan at Hiroshima and Nagasaki. Extensive research led to the development of the

---

*K.M. Panikkar. 1959. *Asia and Western Dominance: The Vasco Da Gama Era in Asia*. UK: George Allen & Unwin Ltd.

hydrogen bomb as well. The thermonuclear race was on. You could not be a Great Power without thermonuclear assets. The Cold War began with USA and its allies—France, Britain and China—on the one side and USSR on the other. Soon, China had the Communist Revolution and the People's Republic of China (PRC) became the first significant ally of USSR. USA refused to recognize the PRC. Nationalist China relegated to the island of Taiwan continued to be a permanent member of the United Nations Security Council (UNSC).

Early on in the post-Cold War period, there was a confrontation between the two camps in Korea, a former colony of Japan which had become liberated but was divided between a communist north and a conservative south. The north invaded the south. The Americans intervened and threw the northern armies back. But then, the Chinese People's Liberation Army (PLA) joined on the side of the north and repulsed the Americans. After four years, peace was negotiated. Korea stayed divided between north and south—North Korea and South Korea—with Americans guaranteeing the military defence of the south. The first round of a military war in the long saga of the Cold War was a draw. Nothing was settled.

For the West, the challenge was to avoid a repetition of the interwar contest as to which system delivered prosperity. Luckily, the work done by John Maynard Keynes and the international monetary system constructed by USA and UK gave the capitalist countries the tools to deliver full employment, sustained growth and mass prosperity for the first time since the advent of the Industrial Revolution in the late eighteenth century.

The Cold War was about acquiring mutual nuclear deterrence which cost each side a lot. It also became an ideological battle between the liberal democratic countries and the communist nations, or the free world and the totalitarian world. Another way to describe it was the exploitative capitalist system which relied on the resources of their present and former colonies as against the people's democracies which supported the liberation movement of the oppressed nations. Some countries led by India set up a movement of non-aligned nations, but the dominant story was the Cold War.

Western Europe, now safely under the American nuclear umbrella, thanks to the North Atlantic Treaty Organization (NATO), began a bold experiment to build a union. France and Germany realized that it was their propensity to fight each other that had plunged the world twice into a war during the twentieth century. They came together along with the Netherlands, Belgium, Luxembourg and Italy and signed the Treaty of Rome in 1957 to form the European Economic Community (EEC) or what became known as the Common Market. This was a customs union which allowed tariff-free trade within, and with tariff on imports from outside. It was to grow over the next half-century into the EU, covering twenty-eight nations.

A Clarion Call

Capitalism prospered for the first thirty years after 1945. The Cold War, which had an initial quiet phase during the years since the Korean War, was heightened when Kennedy became the president in 1961. His inaugural speech gave a hint of the times to come:

> Let every nation know that whether it wishes us well or ill that we shall pay any price, bear any burden, meet any hardship, support any friend, oppose any foe in order to assure the success and survival of liberty.

This was a notice that the battle was going to intensify on ideological as much as the military level. John F. Kennedy's inaugural address was almost a manifesto of the LO. It combined an argument for development and removal of poverty, the propagation of more democratic regimes and the promotion of human rights. But this was covered with a notice that the West was ready for combat and can defeat the rival system. It would win not because of military might alone, but because it championed liberty for all. Of course, the reality of the Cold War meant much deviation from the ideal. USA supported many dictators across the world as long as they signed up for military alliance. It supported apartheid in South Africa and its European allies, such as Portugal, France and Belgium, which were reluctant to give up their colonies. Even so, everyone knew that the free world was capitalist and favoured democracy most of the time.

The Soviet Union had lost twenty-five million people in the Second World War. It could be said with some justice that it bore the brunt of the war against Hitler after 1941, while Great Britain held the fort in the first two years. It secured the countries of Eastern Europe on its border and turned them into communist regimes with state-controlled economies. It believed that it was creating the future order based on the ideas of Marx and Lenin. Many in the Third World (neither with USA nor with USSR) were attracted by the ideals of communism which believed in equality and absence of capitalist exploitation. The Soviet Union could point to the racial inequality in USA and the continuing colonial empires of the masters of the free world. It took the role of the nation, which would befriend all the struggles of the peoples in colonies against their European imperial masters.

The Soviet Union also had problems within its camp. There were uprisings in the German Democratic Republic (East Germany) and Hungary during the 1950s, which were ruthlessly suppressed. Its relations with China soured during the late 1950s. Its encouragement of communist parties across the world was always a source of tension in its international diplomatic transactions. Indonesia suppressed a revolution attempted by the Communist Party of Indonesia (PKI) with excessive violence. Malaya had to suppress a communist insurgency with British help before it could become fully independent. India had to overcome a peasant uprising led by the communist party in the region of Telangana and from the 1960s onward faced a Maoist guerrilla movement. While the Soviet Union was often a friend of the Third World, it was looking to recruit them to its own camp by fomenting a communist takeover.

Kennedy's challenge soon saw concrete evidence. In nearby Cuba, where Castro had led a communist revolution, the likelihood that the Soviet Union could park nuclear missiles led to the most serious confrontation between the two superpowers. The world came very close to nuclear Armageddon, which had been the nightmare of the post-1945 world. Luckily, the episode ended peacefully and led to some detente in the Cold War.

But the Cold War continued. America had been stung by the Soviet Union's lead in the space race. Kennedy made it a national goal to land a man on the moon. The space race was peaceful, but persists to this day. It has military implications, of course, in terms of the capability of launching and delivering long-range missiles.

It's the Economy, Stupid!

It was the economy which finally proved to be the Achilles heel for the Soviet Union. While it could achieve economic growth, it proved incapable of innovations which could improve the quality of life of its citizens, since its best technology was confined primarily to the military–industrial complex. The burden of the space race and the new weaponry, such as intercontinental ballistic missiles (ICBMs) and other long-range missile systems, proved to be too much for the Soviet Union. It began to falter in its economic performance during the 1970s.

In the West, the twenty-five years of sustained prosperity came to an end as well. On the one hand, continuous full employment had strengthened the power of the workers and their trade unions as against the employers. Governments were committed to maintaining full employment by increasing public spending if a recession occurred. The old orthodoxy of balanced budgets had been replaced by an active fiscal policy which used the budget to manage the economy as near to full capacity as possible. Inflation began to be noticeable soon. Its persistence puzzled economists and politicians who had all been weaned on Keynesian economics.

America had its own problems. It had begun to send soldiers to fight in Vietnam, which was formerly a part of the Indo-China ruled by the French. During the Second World War, the Japanese had thrown the French out of Indo-China. After the war, French rule was restored with the help of the British Indian Army. But soon nationalist forces, which had resisted the Japanese, resumed their struggle to throw the French out. In 1954, the French admitted defeat and left. Elections could have been held and the National

Liberation Front led by Ho Chi Minh would have won. But the Cold War intervened. Ho was a communist, and the Americans insisted on the partition of Vietnam into north (communist) and south (free).

Beginning in the 1960s, American involvement became deeper, and soon, America was fighting a proxy war with the Soviet Union and China (despite differences between the two). After Kennedy's assassination in November 1963, President Lyndon B. Johnson continued to pursue the war. This was to cost resources. But America also had problems at home. Americans had fought a bloody civil war in the previous century on the issue of slavery and its continued existence within the union. Slavery had been abolished but the condition of Black Americans was poor. They faced discrimination in housing, education and employment. They were poor and had shorter and more insecure lives. White Americans had begun to become aware of the injustice. Black Americans had fought in the Second World War; they were visible in sports too and were regarded to have skills as good as White Americans; they were prominent in entertainment though not treated as equal.

Lyndon Johnson committed himself to pass civil rights legislation. He also became aware that there was poverty among White as well as Black Americans. He promised to build the 'Great Society', an American version of the European welfare state.

Full employment combined with the Vietnam War and the Great Society led to large trade deficits. America was living beyond its means. At the end of the war, Americans, along with the British, had created architecture for post-war exchange rates between currencies. All currencies were exchanged against the dollar at a fixed ratio. The dollar was to be convertible into gold at $35 to the ounce, but only in official settlement of deficits between countries. As American trade deficits rose, nations found they had dollars in their reserve. They wanted to convert the surplus dollars into gold. The French were especially of the view that gold would be a sounder investment than dollars.

America had the largest stock of gold. But it decided that it could not sustain to buy back dollars at $35 an ounce. On 15 August 1971, President Richard Nixon announced that America would no longer be willing to change dollars for gold. It was unilaterally reneging on its commitment. The world had been, in one way or the other, basing its currencies on a gold standard for three hundred years. Until 1914, the Bank of England guaranteed the price of gold in terms of pound sterling (£3.17 shillings and 9 pence or £3.88 or $18.66 at the then prevailing exchange rate of $4.76 per pound). This price was fixed by Sir Isaac Newton and had been constant for three hundred years. The British went off the gold standard in 1914 and did not return till 1925. The Americans were de facto in charge, and in January 1934, President Roosevelt fixed the price of gold in dollar at $35 per ounce, thus depreciating the currency. In 1945, the Americans reaffirmed the price on which the Bretton Woods system was constructed, but that only lasted twenty-six years.

Once currencies lost their anchor, there was no rule as to how much currency a country could print. Exchange rates became variable, and soon a very active market developed in foreign exchange trade. With no control on how much money could be printed, inflation rose faster than its already increasing rate through the 1960s. Then, in October 1973, the Organization of Petroleum Exporting Countries (OPEC) increased the price of oil fourfold from $3 per barrel to $12. Inflation threatened to go out of control. As inflation rose, workers demanded higher wages. If granted, the higher wages would lead to even higher prices as the wage rise was passed on. In many cases, governments had to choose to control inflation by letting unemployment rise.

The golden quarter-century of full employment was over. Advanced capitalist countries struggled with the task of delivering full employment with price stability. It proved difficult. A decade of stagflation (inflation with high unemployment) followed. The dominance of Keynesian thinking was challenged. Ideas of monetarism—the need to control money supply as a cure for inflation—became popular.

The Theocratic Democracy of Iran

The oil shock was administered by Iran which was among the leading oil-exporting countries. Western countries had been using Iran's oil since its discovery in the early twentieth century. Indeed Iran, though formally independent throughout its history, was treated very much like its protectorate by Britain before the Second World War and by USA afterwards. Iran was to deliver the first rude shock to Western hegemony in the decade of stagflation. To understand its importance, we need to examine Iran's history in some depth.

Iran is a country with a continuous history going back several millennia. It gave birth to Zoroastrianism, but the practitioners of the religion had to leave Iran and migrate to India where they have flourished as Parsis. Iran became the leading Shi'a country in the world. The Safavid dynasty (1501–1750) was parallel to the Mughal dynasty (1526–1857) in India. It was the Safavid dynasty which made Shi'a Islam the national religion of Iran.

Humayun, the son of the founder of the Mughal dynasty, Babur, after his defeat at the hands of a local Afghan king, had to spend fifteen years in exile. It was during this period that he was in Iran, and close relations developed between the two countries. Indian art and culture as it flourished under the Mughals was deeply influenced by the Iranian example.

The Safavid Empire gave way to the Qajar dynasty in the late eighteenth century, which ruled till the early twentieth century. Iran's modern history begins with Reza Shah, a military officer who seized power from the ruling dynasty in 1925. He founded the Pahlavi dynasty. Oil, meanwhile, had been discovered in Iran in the early years of the twentieth century, and the British company Anglo-Persian Oil Company* developed the oilfields and delivered royalties at 16 per cent of its profits. This was never adequate and remained a topic of dispute, but it did keep Iran in tolerable financial condition. Reza Shah spent a lot of that money on building up his army.

Iran's history had oscillated between autocratic kings ruling unchecked and then being confronted and occasionally defeated by the crowds of students from schools and colleges, merchants from the bazaar and the Shi'a clergy. In 1906, there was a democratic uprising against the Qajar dynasty. After five years of on-and-off agitation, the crowds succeeded in achieving democratic change, which created an elected Parliament, Majlis. During the Second World War, Reza Pahlavi was forced to retire when the Allies took control of Iran. The country's importance as a source of oil was vital. The British wanted to control Iran to protect their investment in the Anglo-Persian Oil Company (now renamed Anglo Iranian Oil Company). Reza

---

*This was renamed Anglo Iranian Oil Company in 1935, and is now known as British Petroleum.

Pahlavi abdicated and left the throne to his son. The post-war years saw Mohammad Reza Pahlavi, the successor, challenged again. The popularly elected Prime Minister Mohammad Mossadegh wanted to nationalize the Anglo Iranian Oil Company. But yet again, the Cold War and oil combined to give the Americans a reason to foment a coup to remove Mossadegh. The young Mohammad Reza Pahlavi was restored to his arbitrary power by the Allies.

The young king acquired confidence and was a leader among the oil-exporting countries when they decided to quadruple the price of oil. Iran's revenue also quadrupled. Its share of profits was 50 per cent now. The Shah invested the money in armaments, but also to modernize and industrialize Iran. Between 1960 and 1978, Iran's rate of Gross Domestic Product (GDP) was almost 6 per cent, three times its usual pace. There was also land reform and much migration from the rural areas into the cities of Tehran, Isfahan and others. The 'White Revolution', as the Shah called his reforms, was not popular with everyone. The bazaar was unhappy because imports became affordable and took away local business. The clergy frowned upon modernization and Westernization. Student population had grown enormously from the expansion of education, but, as usual, youth unrest could not be controlled. The Shah had insisted on a single party in Parliament under his control, but he could not control the streets of Tehran.

Ayatollah Khomeini had been a leading cleric and a critic of the Shah over the years. He had been exiled by the Shah in 1963 after one of the more riotous episodes upon which he went to Iraq, but he continued his tirade against the monarchy even during exile. Then again in 1978, the Shah insisted that Iraq expel Khomeini. Ayatollah Khomeini could not be restrained; he went to Paris and continued his criticism against the Shah.

It was in 1979 that the Pahlavi dynasty finally came to an end. Once again, the combination of students, the bazaar and the Shi'a clergy, spearheaded by Ayatollah Khomeini who returned to the country from exile, led the revolution. Iran became a republic but was now ruled by the collective of Shi'a clergy, who chose the supreme leader. America's role in the dismissal of Mossadegh was not forgotten. The large oil fortunes which Iran had been spending had also attracted Americans as contractors, consultants and controllers. Resentment of America took the form of Iranian students laying siege to the American embassy in Tehran. Fresh from its defeat in Vietnam and the hurried retreat from its Saigon embassy, America was faced with another challenge. President Jimmy Carter was approaching the end of his first term and was caught unprepared for this crisis.

It took Ronald Reagan and a short passage of time before the siege was lifted. But Iran succeeded in not only cocking a snook at the great power but also regaining its much valued independence from outside control. The millennia-old kingdom was now an Islamic republic, the first Shi'a republic in history. It fashioned for itself a unique model of theocratic democracy where the collegium of Shi'a clergy determine which candidates get to contest elections, retain a decisive voice in the choice of nominations for the presidency and play a large role in deciding government policy. America and the LO had to learn to cope with this unusual form of democracy. Instead of the one-party rule prevalent in communist democracies, here was a country controlled by a high-level clergy.

America's attitude was to remain hostile to the Islamic republic. Its allies in the region, the Arab nations, never got along with the non-Arab Iranians. America encouraged them to combat Iran. The Iran–Iraq war, which began within a year of the establishment of the Islamic republic in September 1980, was to last eight years and was one of the bloodiest wars in history. It barely attracted attention in the West, and no attempt was made by the UN or any other body to stop the war. The reason, of course, was that USA was behind Saddam Hussein, the ruler of Iraq, who was willing to be armed and aided by the Americans.

The Iranian republic survived the long war with Iraq. It continues to be a theocratic democracy with regular free elections. There are contestations among rival parties in elections. Tension continues between orthodox and reformist trends. In the latest election in 2017, Hassan Rouhani was re-elected as president against a candidate who was reputed to be the protégé of the supreme leader. It has achieved economic prosperity and a capacity to acquire nuclear weapons. It has faced severe sanctions for trying to produce a nuclear weapon. But then, it was the first nation among middle-eastern countries to try for nuclear status on its own. (Israel does have nuclear capability, but this has not been publicly acknowledged.)

The peculiar sensitivities of the Shi'a clergy became evident to the LO when the Iranian clergy declared a fatwa on the life of author Salman Rushdie for what they took to be his blasphemous novel *The Satanic Verses*. Here was a gesture so contrary to liberal sentiments that the LO was shocked all over the world. But many countries with a large Muslim population (such as India which is a liberal democracy) reacted sympathetically to Iran and were hostile to Rushdie. The fatwa has still not been suspended.

The LO was to have further encounters with Islam but that was much later.

Capitalism Reinvents Itself

The problems of stagflation posed a fundamental challenge to governments of the West as they did to the USSR. But while the Soviet Union proved incapable of reinventing itself, capitalism succeeded in renewing itself. The liberal democratic order had a left-wing colouring through the first thirty years after the war. The influence of the New Deal* had made the activist state respectable. There was a bipartisan consensus in America as in Western Europe (though with a more explicit socialist influence) that the state had to run the economy to guarantee full employment, and in Europe, even own and run some industries and finance a welfare state.

As stagflation took hold, this consensus broke down. In USA, as well as in UK and Germany, politicians came to power who abandoned the statist consensus and reaffirmed the importance of free markets and control of inflation by adopting monetary and fiscal discipline. Ronald Reagan, Margaret Thatcher and Helmut Kohl set the new agenda. The ideas of monetarism popularized by Milton Friedman and even the older libertarian ideas of Friedrich Hayek became fashionable again. Statism retreated and capitalism reinvented itself by making business profitable. Restrictions on prices and industries were relaxed. Many nationalized industries were privatized in UK.

The effect of stagflation in the 1970s had been to encourage the relocation of manufacturing to markets where cheaper labour could be hired. There had been innovations such as the container

---

*The New Deal was a series of programmes, including, most notably, Social Security, that were enacted in USA between 1933 and 1938, and a few that came later.

ship and the Comsat which facilitated the relocation of factories and management at a distance. Many industries moved to Asia. There were soon talks of Asian tigers and newly industrializing economies of Asia. Hong Kong, Singapore, Taiwan and South Korea became miracle economies. Japan had already showed that it could become a pioneer in electronic technology and grew at unprecedented rates from the 1960s onwards. The centre of gravity of manufacturing began to move eastwards.

Although many did not realize this, this relocation landed a body blow to the traditional industrial working class in the West. The manufacturing jobs, which guaranteed round-the-year employment with overtime, steadily rising wages and lifetime guarantee of work, were soon gone. In USA, manufacturing jobs as a percentage of non-farm payroll peaked at 22 per cent in 1977. They have been declining ever since. By 2012, the number was just 9 per cent. Unskilled and semi-skilled manual workers who had good jobs found themselves thrown into lower-paid service sector jobs. Wages stopped growing in America and have not grown for forty years. This was the most long-lasting influence on the formation of the discontented white working class which caught everyone's attention when Trump got elected. Of course, Black Americans had just been able to get manufacturing jobs when the bottom fell out. Thus, they also suffered, but they had never seen the good days to regret the loss. It was different with the white workers in America. In Europe, deindustrialization led to many people becoming unemployed over the long term with limited chance of re-employment. But the welfare state was more generous in Europe than in USA.

Finance Takes Over

The industries which remained in the West were the high-tech ones that employed educated and skilled workers. The premium on education increased as good jobs required college education. But Western economies, especially USA and UK, also financialized while they deindustrialized. The simultaneous arrival of information technology innovations and the many more new products from Silicon Valley transformed the nature of work. UK inaugurated a dynamic financial market with the city of London abandoning its old oligopolistic culture and embracing competition and innovation. This was the Big Bang.* The workforce in London's financial market became international and cosmopolitan.

The Western capitalist economies rebounded after twenty years of low growth and inflation. The 1970s were dire. Recovery began after a tough fight against inflation and the shrinking of the welfare state during the 1980s. In the second half of the 1980s, President Ronald Reagan delivered a growing economy thanks to tax cuts, supply-side reforms and some old-fashioned military spending.

Western Europe had spent the same time searching for an anchor for its currencies. Leaders of France and Germany along with the other original members of EEC wanted stability in their foreign exchange markets. They sought to limit the variation among their currencies by adopting limits to devaluations against each other.

---

*The phrase 'Big Bang', used in reference to the sudden deregulation of financial markets, was coined to describe measures, including abolition of fixed commission charges and of the distinction between stockjobbers and stockbrokers in the London Stock Exchange and change from open-outcry to electronic, screen-based trading, effected by Margaret Thatcher in 1986.

Their search was to lead to a single currency which was adopted by the end of the century. But much else had changed by then.

The end of the 1980s saw the fall of the Berlin Wall, which was a symbol of the oppressive regimes in Eastern Europe. Soon the reunification of Germany was on the cards after forty-five years of division. But a much bigger dividend was due to the West. USSR, once the beacon of the future utopia, disintegrated without a shot being fired by the West. No one, not even the Central Intelligence Agency (CIA) and the most virulent Cold Warriors, had expected a peaceful dissolution of the 'Evil Empire'.

The proximate cause of the collapse was insufficient reform of the highly centralized economic and political system by Mikhail Gorbachev, who became the general secretary of the Communist Party of the Soviet Union (CPSU) in 1985. He liberalized the political life by his policy of 'glasnost'—openness. But the monopoly of the CPSU remained. The economy was not reformed even marginally to absorb market institutions. Gorbachev antagonized the hard-line elite in the CPSU. He decentralized political power by converting the Union of Soviet Socialist Republics into the Union of Soviet *Sovereign* Republics. This did lead to the hardliners staging a coup during August 1991 while Gorbachev was abroad. Yeltsin, the Russian leader, defied the coup by recruiting the army. Gorbachev was powerless to resist the decision by the republics of Russia, Ukraine and Belarus to assert their independence of USSR. They had a constitutional right to do so. Soon, other republics joined them. USSR was replaced by the Commonwealth of Independent States (CIS). It had been less than six months since the coup.

The Sole Superpower

With the demise of the USSR, the best phase of the LO began. USA was the sole superpower. The dispute which began in 1945 was settled. Liberal democratic capitalism had won against the Leninist alternative. A gigantic experiment of testing rival systems of running an economy had been carried out in real time and with real people from 1917 to 1991. Capitalism had won. John Kennedy's challenge of assuring 'the survival and success of liberty' had been met. The lily was gilded further for the LO when apartheid came to an end as the official policy in South Africa with a pact between F.W. De Klerk and Nelson Mandela (winning them jointly the Nobel Peace Prize). Mandela, who had spent decades in Robben Island prison, emerged as a great global hero of the late twentieth century.

USA became a champion of human rights which had been an issue of ideological football between the rival camps. The need to shore up friendly dictators was gone, so promoting democracy everywhere became a plank of US foreign policy. The EU was of the same view. As countries began to apply to join the Union, mainly from Eastern Europe, the EU laid down preconditions about democratic elections, rule of law and human rights. It had grown from the initial six to twelve by the mid-1970s and then fifteen by the 1990s. Soon it was to grow to twenty-five. Now it stands at twenty-eight. The LO was spreading its wings.

In domestic politics, there came about a convergence of ideologies with free market ideas taking the lead and left parties embracing the notion that the economy had to be well run (on capitalist lines) to secure progressive policies. President Bill Clinton heralded this consensus by reforming the welfare state to prune public spending.

He also deregulated financial markets and relaxed the sixty-year-old restrictions on banking in the Glass–Steagall Act passed during the New Deal years. In UK, Prime Minister Tony Blair refashioned the British Labour Party to embrace the policies of Margaret Thatcher with an added progressive brush. Ideological differences became narrow or non-existent.

At the same time, thanks to efforts stretching twenty years back, a new global regime of free trade was negotiated in the form of a treaty. It established the World Trade Organization (WTO), which introduced a uniform set of rules for trade between nations which would guarantee a level playing field. Financial markets were now free and versatile enough to be able to move capital anywhere around the world. The collapse of the USSR meant the liberation of East European economies from statist control. They acquired financial markets and other capitalist institutions. For the first time since 1917, capitalism became the only game in towns around the world, except for a small number of countries such as North Korea and Cuba.

This happy coincidence of USA being the sole superpower, the institutional structure to guarantee free trade and a decade of relative prosperity was celebrated as the climax of the LO. Francis Fukuyama acknowledged it as *The End of History and the Last Man*, which actually meant the Hegelian goal of the Triumph of Reason—the full realization of their own rationality by human beings. It was the climax of the evolution of human consciousness. There was no further progress possible. Others speculated that we were living in a borderless world or that the Earth was flat. The early 1990s were the years when it seemed promises were delivered. The communist utopia may have failed to arrive, but capitalism was delivering its best.

Perhaps the most remarkable development was in the way language recognized the dignity of people. There was a 'politically correct' language. Those who were slaves once were no longer called Negroes or even 'coloured people', a description one of their progressive associations, the National Association for the Advancement of the Colored People, had chosen. They were to be called African Americans and later Black Americans. Women's movement for equality of social regard was powered by feminism which struggled from the 1960s onwards to change the language and the attitude of men as they interacted with women. Later, the freedom of people to choose their lifestyle as gay or lesbian or their gender identity as transgender or bisexual was secured. The struggle for social equality along all these dimensions is by no means over, but the discourse has been transformed. All this, of course, relates to the public behaviour of the members of the LO. There are still areas of darkness. But the world arrived at a cultural milestone of acknowledging the equality of all.

That said, we should not delude ourselves that real equality has come just because the language has improved. Women still get paid less for the same work as men do, have insecure jobs and do not get chosen for the seats at the top table. They suffer from domestic violence and sexual harassment. Black Americans are socially and economically poorer than their white or Hispanic counterparts. Black Americans are in disproportionately large numbers in American prisons, and, as the Black Lives Matter movement has reminded us, they face death at the hands of the forces of law. The inequality of income is hardly the worst. The daily lives of people living within and even more on the periphery of the LO reflect a whole host of of inequalities. There is much more to do.

Even so, the world had not stopped changing. Capitalism was to transform the world in ways that had not been foreseen. The geography of capitalism was changing even though history may have come to an end. But history had not come to a full stop. The rules of dialectics would reassert themselves. The powerful were sowing the seeds of their own weakening. It would soon turn out that the most powerful part of their economies—the financial sector—would prove to be the weak spot.

Ever Closer Europe

For Western Europe, the urgent task was to overcome age-old national rivalries and build a future on the confident (though not necessarily safe) assumption that wars were a thing of the past. A Kantian ideal world of universal peace was upon Europe, and a new world had to be built. From the Treaty of Rome which established an economic community of six, the rapid and remarkable recovery of Western Europe (some thanks to Marshall Aid and American soldiers on European soil) attracted other countries. UK applied as early as 1961, but was only accepted in 1972 as a member. By the time of the fall of the Berlin Wall, the momentum was behind the EEC. There were fifteen members soon and the European Community began its journey to become a European Union.

One ideal was border-free movement across the community. The Schengen Treaty provides that citizens of member countries can move within the community visa free. The ideal was an ever closer union. The EEC had become the European Community and now would be the European Union. It would not just be a customs union with tariff-free trade within its boundaries, but become a single market with free movement of capital, goods and services as well as people.

The EU has evolved for itself a unique constitutional arrangement. The executive body is the European Commission which frames the common set of rules and regulations. The Commission consists of the nominated representatives of member countries. These 'commissioners' are senior politicians of their countries and have a five-year tenure. There is a council, where heads of government meet to decide on major policy issues. The president of the Commission is chosen by the council. There is a parliament which used to have nominated members, but has now evolved to having directly elected members. The parliament does not elect the executive nor is the council accountable to the parliament. This has led to frequent complaints that the rulers in the EU are unelected.

The EU is a bold experiment. Its most peculiar feature is an almost total absence of a central government. The Commission is an unelected executive body. The public finances are also unique. There is no common taxation, though every member country has value added tax (VAT), though at different rates, and there is no facility for fiscal transfers. The EU budget is around 1.25 per cent of the EU GDP. Thus, the Union is neither a federation nor a confederation. It may become one or the other, but that is for the future.

The most ambitious project of the Union was the adoption of a single currency. Upon the abandonment of the gold–dollar link by USA, the European Community began a search for an alternative anchor which would avoid flexible, and, in its view, unstable exchange rates and harness the community in another system of fixed exchange rates. There had to be a European monetary system independent of the dollar. By the 1990s, after experiments with other arrangements to tie the currencies together, a single currency (later to be called the euro) was proposed in the Maastricht Treaty. This was to be a disciplined regime wherein individual members promised to maintain their debt-to-GDP ratio below 60 per cent and keep deficits under control—below 3 per cent of GDP—and maintain open capital markets. UK secured an exemption from the single currency, as did Denmark. Recent entrants to the EU from Eastern Europe will have to wait a while for their acceptance into the euro. But all willing members of the EU who were eligible on the debt and deficit criteria joined. Today, there are nineteen members. The European Central Bank (ECB) is not allowed to buy government debt of any member country in the primary market. This in effect means that no country can borrow to fund the deficit by selling their bonds to the central bank. The bonds have to be bought by private agents, including commercial banks.

The euro is a unique currency. It is like the gold standard inasmuch as no country can unilaterally devalue nor expand its own money supply, except through private banks lending money to private investors or in limited fashion to governments. It is a highly deflationary arrangement. The reason for this is that the German economy suffered from hyperinflation in the 1920s and ever since has eschewed monetary expansion as a way out of difficulties. After the war, when the German Federal Republic was established (in West Germany), the Bundesbank, its central bank, was given a mandate to abandon monetary financing of government debt. (Only rarely has the Bundesbank bought government bonds to smooth flows of credit.) Germany maintained an orthodox monetary and fiscal policy which laid the foundations of its prosperity. As a leading architect of the Union, its stance on monetary orthodoxy has prevailed. A member of the Eurozone has no control over the exchange rates, no influence over the interest rate set by the ECB and limited ability to run a budget deficit, though countries have tried to stretch this limit as best as they can get away with.

The Balkan Nightmare

While the European Community was building its structure to become a union where wars were banished and the rule of law was to prevail among nations, there was a rude shock delivered to the LO by developments in southeastern Europe. The word 'Balkans', so loved by the nineteenth-century liberals, was back in use.

Yugoslavia was a collection of separate kingdoms of a variety of Slav people—Serbs, Bosnians, Croatians and Slovene—who were under the Ottoman Empire and then taken over by the Austro-Hungarian Empire. It was a Serb nationalist, Gavrilo Princip, who assassinated Archduke Ferdinand of Austria which triggered reactions leading to the First World War. At the end of the war, a kingdom of Serbs, Croats and Slovene was recognized in international treaties. During the Second World War when the Axis powers invaded the kingdom, a resistance movement led by Joseph Broz Tito defended the kingdom. After the war, Tito founded the Federal People's Republic of Yugoslavia. He was a communist but soon broke with Stalin and occupied a mid-position between the two Cold War camps. It was Tito along with Jawaharlal Nehru and Egypt's Gamal Abdel Nasser who founded the Non-Aligned Movement (NAM).

Yugoslavia under Tito became the envy of many socialists. It seemed to avoid the cruelties of Stalinist USSR and the problems of capitalism. There was workers' ownership rather than state ownership, and more freedom than in many communist countries. It was hailed as the Third Way.

But the federation had tensions mainly due to the unequal size of the units and the mixture of different communities which were potentially nationalities. After Tito's death, tensions about governance increased. Serbia, the largest unit, had only one vote among the six units, but it also had provinces—Kosovo being one—which were larger than other units. Eventually, nationalism among the different Slavic communities led to conflict among them. The end of the Cold War and collapse of the USSR had led to all Eastern European countries becoming free to settle their future. Soon conflict broke out between Serbia and Croatia and spread to other units of the federal republic.

The Yugoslav wars were shockingly violent. For Europe, which had thought it had transcended the passions of nationalism, it was a reminder that even within the Slavic people, ethnic differences and real or fancied historical grievances could lead to murderous consequences in the late twentieth century. It required a UN resolution and America's military help to the armed forces of the nations of the European Community to establish ceasefire. War crimes were committed and human rights routinely violated. One could not imagine that somehow we had attained the Kantian ideal of universal peace. Various units of the Federal People's Republic of Yugoslavia became independent nations—Serbia, Croatia, Slovenia, Macedonia, Montenegro, Bosnia–Herzegovina (which has a large Muslim population) and Kosovo.

The Chinese Transformation

China was the best example of the turnaround from a world of competing economic systems to a single dominating one. It had been a communist country. Unlike the proletarian revolution expected in Europe as predicted by Lenin, Mao had led a peasant revolution. Winning power in 1949, the Communist Party of China (CPC) under Mao's leadership had begun to reform Chinese society, removing many old feudal restrictions. But Mao's economic policies were overambitious and based more on fantasy than economics. The policies led to economic ruin and the biggest famine in 1960 that China or the world had seen, claiming forty million victims, though this was not known till nearly thirty years later. Further upheavals followed as Mao launched a cultural revolution, exiling his subordinates and unleashing anarchy on the country. After his death in 1976, Deng Xiaoping, one of his old comrades, seized power and began to change the direction of China's economy. Deng kept the monopoly of the CPC in political decision making but began to introduce capitalist elements into the economy. Unlike Gorbachev, he reformed the economy while leaving power in the hands of the Communist Party. Agriculture, which had been collectivized in communes by Mao, was decentralized by giving land back to householders and allowing them to sell output surplus to state procurement on the free market. Foreign capital and technology were admitted. Soon, China became the world's manufacturing factory. It was the latest Asian tiger.

The change brought about by the advent of the 1990s phase of the LO helped China accelerate its growth. Capital flowed to China from around the world (especially from the Chinese diaspora) to profit from the cheap labour and disciplined workers that the country offered. Soon China was growing at double-digit rates and achieved what Japan had done beginning in the 1960s and South Korea from the 1970s inwards. China grew at an average of 10 per cent for thirty-three years between 1978 and 2011, a record unequalled by any other economy.

It moved from being a developing country to the second largest economy in terms of total income within twenty years of the watershed year of 1990. The global centre of economic gravity was moving eastwards even as the West was basking in its triumph. The mirror image of the growth of manufacturing in China was its decline in the West. US data show a gentle decline in manufacturing jobs from the late 1970s till 1990, and then a steep decline. There is a debate though about the reason for this change—whether it was the freer trade under WTO rules and the resultant trade with China or the stagnation in the US productivity growth. But the perception remains that it was the Chinese ability to provide manufactures at cheaper prices than the rest which did the trick. It was a combination of Chinese savings plus American capital and technology and Chinese labour.

As it happened (though more by accident than design), the global economy had its best two decades in many years. The golden quarter-century of Keynesian economics between 1945 and 1970 had been good for the developed countries, but not for the poor ones. This time around, capital flowed to the periphery. The economies previously labelled 'underdeveloped', 'backward' or 'developing' were now called 'emerging'. India, which had lagged behind in the growth league as it pursued old-fashioned Fabian socialist economic policies, broke with its past in 1991 and began to implement market-friendly reforms. India's left-wing parties, long used to dictating the economic discourse, denounced the new regime as neoliberal. But the result soon showed. India lifted its annual income growth rate from around 3 per cent to 7 per cent. The new LO could truly claim to be global.

There was a phenomenal reduction in the number of people below the poverty line. As would befit a guardian of the global economy, the World Bank had a simple single indicator to define who was poor and who was not. One American dollar per day was the measure. It was modified for different countries taking into account price differences—the so-called Purchasing Power Parity (PPP). Between China and India alone, half a billion people could be defined as no longer poor by that measure.

Of course, scholars disputed whether a dollar was adequate or whether poverty should be measured in terms of income alone. The United Nations Development Programme (UNDP) proposed an alternative measure not so much for individuals or households as for regions and nations. The Human Development Index (HDI) combined life expectancy, literacy and income to construct a measure of performance and ranked nations on a single scale. There was a keen interest in this new index which was (mistakenly) labelled as the Happiness Index. But in basic terms, this was the time when one could talk of the entire globe in terms of a single economy and measure its performance.

A Global Village

It was the best of all possible worlds if you were well off and among the elite in the LO. The whole world was your oyster. You could access your money wherever you were. Travel and tourism became easier.

The economic and political elite discovered a mountain village in Switzerland—Davos—to meet annually and celebrate their success and good fortune. The new products in information technology had made the dissemination of messages easier. There were mobile phones and emails. Now a BlackBerry became the status symbol of the global man (they were still predominantly men) as it combined mobile telephony with emailing. Of course, the competition was such among a small set of companies—an oligopoly—that 'smartphones' became better and cheaper. The privilege of having a smartphone became widespread. Unlike earlier innovations, now the new goods got cheaper as they got better.

Economists had put an end to their quarrels as Keynesians or Monetarists. The Great Moderation prevailed and economists agreed that fiscal policy had to be predictable and cautious in terms of deficits and debts.* Central banks had to be independent of governments and had to ensure a low and stable rate of inflation.

For the developed countries, inflation was low and growth and employment high. This combination of low inflation and full employment was credited to clever central bankers and the economists' Great Moderation. Interest rates were low and money supply grew at a steady pace, but the economy did not overheat. The real reason, however, lay in the nature of the new global economy rather than in the cleverness of bankers. China had entered the global economy, and its four hundred million workers in the manufacturing sector had cheapened manufacturing goods, all of which were exported by China to Western markets.

---

*The Great Moderation refers to a period of economic stability characterized by low inflation, positive economic growth and the belief that the boom and bust cycle had been overcome.

During the 1970s, it was industrial products which were the source of inflation as wages rose faster than productivity. Now the same products coming from Asia were cheap and stayed so. The only other source of inflation was raw material prices—oil, which had lit the fire in 1973, or mineral and agricultural commodities. Through the 1990s, they stayed reasonably steady.

The Asian Crisis

Towards the end of the 1990s, there was a financial crisis, but it was in faraway Asia. As capital was mobile, it went wherever it could find high returns. Thailand was the country which attracted a lot of foreign money in its real estate markets. The Thai currency—the baht—was pegged to the dollar, and so investors believed their investments were safe from exchange rate risk. But rising inflation in Thailand in 1997 made investors uneasy. When they tried to withdraw and repatriate their money, it was revealed that the Thai Central Bank had inadequate reserves to service the outflow. The baht left its dollar peg and depreciated rapidly and drastically. The contagion spread to Malaysia, Indonesia and South Korea. These economies had done nothing wrong, but since they were in Asia, investors began to flee them. The International Monetary Fund (IMF) intervened and set tough conditions before bailing the Asian economies out. The countries never forgot how deep a deflation they had to impose on their poor citizens as a result of IMF conditions.

The Asian crisis spread to Russia and threatened to become global. But the Federal Reserve System showed that it was the world's central bank like the Bank of England used to be. It cut interest rates, eased credit conditions and averted the crisis from becoming global. If anything, this reinforced the feeling of superiority among the rich countries. They had better behaved central banks and better regulated financial markets. This sense of hubris was to cost dear within a few years.

China and India had stayed out of the Asian crisis. They had never signed up to the full liberal policy of open capital markets with fully convertible currency. They had not deregulated their banks. They felt vindicated in their cautious policy. But generally, the message the Asian countries received from this crisis and the IMF's behaviour was that they could not rely on global institutions to come to their help. The world may have become a global village, but they were confined (like the untouchables in Indian villages) to the periphery of the village away from where the masters lived. If they wanted to move in, they had to become rich like the current masters. They had to build up their own reserves. They had to export but not import. Their surplus had to be squirrelled away as reserves. They had to practise mercantilism. Then they would never need to call the IMF to their aid and not be lectured to by foreigners.

Challenge to the LO

The twentieth century thus saw the triumph of USA and the defeat of USSR in the battle for the mastery of the globe. Of course, the globe in everyone's imagination in the LO was just America and Europe. But there was another world out there, a world dominated by European imperialism during the previous two centuries, which was now free and awake. Some of the many colonial subjects had migrated to the 'master' countries and formed the diaspora. Their history with Europe went back farther than just a century. Europeans had written that history as the victors, but neither read nor remembered it. But the vanquished had read that history, and it was drilled into their memory. That defined the next battlefield.

The British, French and Dutch Empires in South and South East Asia had been defeated by the end of the 1950s. In Africa, the same story was to be repeated by the end of the 1960s. The fall of the empires was achieved, sometimes accompanied by bloodshed, as in Belgian Congo. There was a civil war in southern Rhodesia which became Zimbabwe. The Portuguese resisted decolonization, and their empire—Goa, Mozambique and Angola—had to struggle to break free.

The challenge to the superpower status of USA and the triumphant LO came not from the old enemies in communist Europe, but from a totally unexpected source—Islamist jihad. Religion had lost its salience in the LO. The nineteenth-century battles waged by modernity against religion had been forgotten. Religion was there as a benevolent, moderate and decorative presence. The belief was mainly Christian, or, to use the recently coined label, Judaeo-Christian. The merging of the two Biblical faiths was atonement for the horrible memory of the Holocaust. The two-thousand-year history of Christian anti-Semitism had to be wiped out.

Encounters with Islam

Few were aware of the third of the Abrahamic religions—Islam. There had been an astounding movement among Black Americans beginning in Chicago in the late 1950s. Elijah Muhammad had begun preaching and converting black men and women to Islam. His was a message of peace and solidarity. The Nation of Islam (NOI) taught its followers to behave in an exemplary fashion and avoid the usual traps that Black Americans fell into. The most popular and famous follower of Elijah Muhammad was the Black American boxer Cassius Clay, who converted to Islam and adopted the name Muhammad Ali. This had invited much attention to the NOI. Malcolm X was another charismatic follower of Elijah Muhammad; later, however, he left the movement and was assassinated. But all this made little impact on the LO. Few were inspired to learn about the doctrine or practices of Islam. The NOI lived in the ghetto far away from those who inhabited the world of the LO. It was the Christian Church in the south with radical pastors such as Dr Martin Luther King Jr, Reverend Ralph Abernathy and others who had taken the lead in the struggle for Black American civil rights movement. As far as the LO was concerned, Black Americans had won their struggle and their elite had been absorbed. Islam was alien territory.

There had been the painful encounter for America in 1979 when the Shah in Iran was replaced by the Islamic Revolution headed by Ayatollah Khomeini. The American embassy was put under a siege by the angry Shi'a youth for over a year. Iran and Iraq had then fought an eight-year war in which USA supported Saddam Hussein.

However, when the same Saddam invaded Kuwait in 1991, USA, under a UN resolution, put together a coalition of nations under Operation Desert Storm to remove him from Kuwait. Despite much urging, President George H.W. Bush refused to go to Baghdad to replace Saddam. He kept to the UN mandate. It was a rare, if not unique, instance of a permanent member of the UNSC abiding by a UN resolution.

There had been an earlier episode during the final years of the Cold War. The Soviet Union had gone into Afghanistan where the communist party removed the king and formed a government. There were many rival groups in Afghanistan and some across the border in Pakistan which were opposed to the regime. These groups were supported by Pakistan President Zia-ul-Haq. He had been the chief of army staff and had removed the democratically elected Prime Minister Zulfiqar Ali Bhutto and then had him hanged. He wanted to convert Pakistan into an orthodox Islamic nation, enforcing the Sharia and a strict dress code. He was the ally the Americans needed to help fund the rival Afghan groups who would undermine the communist regime in Afghanistan. One group which emerged was the Taliban—meaning 'students' in Pashto. They were purists in their practise of Islam, with no concessions to modernity of any kind, and had a fanatical determination to remove the godless communist regime. The guerrilla armies were furnished with drugs (to sell and earn money) and guns by the Americans.

The Taliban grew to be one of the first powerful Islamist groups. They were puritanical and believed in keeping their women at home without education or entertainment. They were everything which the LO would disapprove of, the latter barely aware that it was the American government which had fed the monster. Some members of the Taliban were diverted towards Pakistan's continuing dispute with India about Kashmir. They formed cross-border terrorist groups. But other groups fanned out further westwards.

It was one such group—the Al Qaeda—which began striking blows to the US presence around the world. The origin of the anti-Americanism of its leader, Osama bin Laden, was in a dispute with the ruling family of Saudi Arabia. They had invited American troops on Saudi soil to provide protection against outside attacks. But this, according to Osama, being the Holy Land of Islam with

Mecca and Medina, the ruling family had desecrated it by having an infidel army on its soil.

Osama came from a rich and prominent Saudi family engaged in the construction business. He began to fight his war against the royal family and through that waged a battle against the Americans. The Saudi royal family had espoused Wahhabism, one of the most puritanical of Islamic sects. It is in complete denial of all forms of modernity and wants to get back to the days when the Prophet preached his gospel. It is misogynistic and disapproves of music and any form of luxury or decoration. It is fanatical in its belief that Islam is the true religion and everyone should convert to it. Osama was of the same sect, but he thought the royal family had deviated from the true path.

The first attack that Al Qaeda planned was on the New York World Trade Center but it was frustrated. This was followed by the attack on USS Cole and later on the American embassy in Kenya. The successful attacks in the 1990s were away from the mainland, and while they attracted attention, their significance was minor. But then, something catastrophic happened as the new millennium arrived.

9/11 and the Birth of a New Age

The attack on the World Trade Center on 11 September 2001 changed the fortunes of the LO and America, the sole superpower. The fifty-year Cold War had been decisively won by USA, and Europe was at peace. It could be said that America had not won the Korean War and had lost in Vietnam. But those reverses were soon forgotten by the triumph that Reagan secured against the real enemy. But here was a new challenge. 9/11 was the first attack on American soil since Pearl Harbor. It was launched by an elusive enemy—an urban guerrilla army. It was a terrorist act. The War on Terror has now occupied the Western world for all the years since 9/11, and there is no end in sight.

To begin with, it was not even clear who the enemy was. The attackers proclaimed the name of Allah and saw their mission as a holy one. But they represented a *political* movement, not a religious one. Islamism had been battling Muslim nations where it thought the governments were not sufficiently Islamic. It was powerful in Algeria where it had won an election, which was annulled. It had a presence in Egypt through the Muslim Brotherhood and it had, after all, defeated the government in Afghanistan. Islamism was a Sunni movement, the majority strand of Islam. The Shi'a, the minority sect, had already shown their power in Iran when Ayatollah Khomeini replaced the Shah with an Islamic republic run by a collective of Ayatollahs.

The shock of 9/11 was profound. Anyone who watched it 'live', as I did by chance (I was tuned to TV news at home, waiting for the British Trade Union Conference to begin where Tony Blair was to make a speech), would never forget it. I saw the second plane ploughing into the towers; it was a chilling moment. History changed its direction then. The onward, upward March of Reason and Liberalism celebrated by Francis Fukuyama, among others, came to a juddering halt. It has been hobbling along since.

With 9/11, the focus of global conflict has shifted towards the Middle East. Of course, the movement is global and has inflicted damage on countries around the world. London was bombed on 7 July 2005 (7/7). Since then, Mumbai, Bali, Paris, Brussels, Boston and many more places have suffered terror attacks. Al Qaeda set up a loose organization in which many outfits could claim to be a part; franchising was relaxed. The structure had Osama bin Laden at its head (now it is Ayman al-Zawahiri). But it is even more a message for others to follow its example. Entry into the terror business is easy. Many young people who do not value their life or seriously believe in rewards after death promised in the Koran (or so they are led to believe) are willing to become terrorists. It is not a territorial battle, nor is there anyone with whom a truce could be negotiated.

The Perennial War on Terror

For the Americans, the arrival of an enemy which defies destruction is annoying. The sole superpower is being constantly challenged. Although President Obama sanctioned the pursuit and killing of Osama bin Laden, which was achieved successfully, the war has only moved elsewhere. To understand why this is so we have to go back, once again, to a century ago.

The First World War settled the fate of many European empires. The Romanov Empire succumbed to the Bolshevik Revolution. The Habsburg Empire dissolved into many independent nations— Austria, Hungary and Czechoslovakia, among others. The German emperor, the kaiser, abdicated and the Weimar Republic took his place. In a way, the problems created by this dissolution, especially of Germany, led to the Second World War. Then, the unresolved issues of that war led to the Cold War, which only ended in 1991 with the collapse of the USSR.

But there was another empire which was defeated: the Ottoman, the Islamic empire that straddled Europe and Asia. The emperor, the sultan, claimed direct descent from the Prophet. The dynasty derived its name from Uthman, the third caliph (644–656 CE), who had known the Prophet during his lifetime. The first four caliphs who had known the Prophet personally are known as Rashidun (the rightly guided). After the demise of the Prophet, the Muslim armies built, one after another, empires headed by the descendants of one or the other of the original caliphs or members of the Prophet's family. The Ottoman Empire lasted from 1299 till 1923, longer than any other European empire. The Ottoman was the last of the Islamic empires tracing their connection to the Prophet. The sultan was a spiritual head of the Sunni Muslim community (Ummah) and prayers would be offered to him every Friday in mosques around the world wherever Sunni Muslims prayed.

The British came to the defence of the Ottoman Empire in the Crimean War against Russia. In the First World War, the Ottoman Empire had joined the Axis powers. The defeat of the Ottoman Empire was anticipated. The British and the French made a secret treaty known as the Sykes–Picot Agreement, named after the diplomats on the two sides who drafted it. This treaty divided up the Ottoman Empire among the two Allies. Syria and Lebanon went to the French, while Iraq and Jordan were in the British sphere as was Palestine. The Bolsheviks published the secret treaty as soon as they came to power, thus embarrassing the British and the French. Still, that was the map of post-war settlement.

It is difficult for others to comprehend the deep shock suffered by the Sunni Ummah around the world at the end of the empire, which was the last link connecting the present to the Prophet. It was as if the pope had been removed permanently from Rome. There was no undisputed spiritual leader of Sunni Islam now. There were rumours that the British may choose a new caliph or even abolish the caliphate. Mahatma Gandhi led a movement in India to protest against that possibility. But it was not the British who decided the future of the caliphate. The caliphate was abolished by Mustafa Kemal Pasha, who led Turkey after the dissolution of the Ottoman Empire. Kemal Pasha wanted to modernize, indeed Westernize, Turkey and he thought religion was an obstacle to the country's progress. He established a secular republic with the army as a protector of the constitution.

The jolt suffered at the end of the caliphate was multiplied by the decision to assign the control of Jerusalem to the British. The holy city of Islam (as well as Christians and Jews) was thus going to be occupied by the infidels, the lot defeated during the Crusades. To add to this, the British, in the Balfour Declaration in 1917, promised the leaders of the Zionist movement that Jews could make their home in Palestine, with the caveat that they must respect the rights of the people who had already settled there—the Palestinians. But the centenary of the Balfour Declaration was not be universally celebrated in the Middle East because the state of Israel was set up following a UN resolution after the Second World War. This, as far as the Arab nations of the region were concerned, was an anathema. Palestine had Jerusalem, which had the Al-Aqsa mosque associated with the Prophet. This was intolerable.

The Arab countries attempted to destroy Israel leading to three wars in 1948, 1967 and 1973, all of which Israel won. After the first defeat, there had been a lot of churning in the Middle East. The kingdoms which had been set up in the territories of the Ottoman Empire in Iraq, Syria and Jordan faced democratic resistance. Syria and Iraq got rid of their monarchies, replacing them with a populist dictatorship. The Ba'ath Party, an Arab socialist party, was successful in Syria and Iraq. Egypt, also a monarchy, became a republic after an army revolt, with Gamal Abdel Nasser as the president. He had socialist inclinations and believed in pan-Arab unity. He wanted to unite Arab countries under the banner of the United Arab Republic. The promise of a modernized socialist Arabia was very much on the cards by the early 1960s. But the Arab armies lost again to Israel in 1967, followed by another defeat in 1973.

After 1973, the pan-Arab movement in its secular, socialist form lost its credibility only to be replaced by an intense religiosity, especially the Wahhabi message propagated by the oil-rich Saudi regime. Modernity had failed the Arabs. They went back to the tried and true religion. This is, of course, a simplification. There were regimes such as Iraq and Syria which were 'secular', but their Sunni/Shi'a orientation was not in doubt.

The Middle East has been at war more or less continuously since 1973, though this was among the Muslim nations. The war which began in 2001 after the attack on the twin towers has still not ended. During the course, though Al Qaeda has been reduced and Osama bin Laden has been killed, the organization has not been eliminated. It is not even clear what elimination of such a guerrilla movement would mean. The Taliban has been contained and an Afghan civilian government has been established, but even so, Afghanistan remains less than secure. This war has lasted longer than the Vietnam War and there is no sense of closure.

Then, in 2003, George Bush and Tony Blair decided that Saddam Hussein was a major threat to the West as he had weapons of mass destruction (WMD) and had to be eliminated. While Saddam was removed and hanged, the restoration of Iraq to a properly governed country had taken much longer. There was a serious falling out between USA and UK on the one side and the EU countries on the other about the legitimacy of the war. UK had tried to get a UN resolution passed to reinforce an earlier resolution which justified armed intervention in Iraq. But France opposed it as a permanent member of the Security Council. Various undiplomatic insults were exchanged between the American 'Neocons' (neoconservatives) and the Europeans. Eastern European countries were praised as the New Europe supportive of tough action and Old Europe was derided.

Iraq also dented the liberal reputation of Tony Blair and, in the longer run, split and demoralized the Labour Party. New Labour, Blair's attempt to create an ideology-free centre-left party, dissolved and sharper ideological differences reappeared in British politics. Europe was temporarily alienated from USA. It was only when Barack Obama was elected the president that Europe cheered up. The award of the Nobel Prize for Peace to Obama in 2009 was more a sign of Europe's relief that America had chosen a liberal, even a Black American, as the president than any achievements of Obama as a peacemaker. The prize was mainly for not being George Bush, and only secondarily for being Obama.

The Neocons had a hegemonic dream of making the Middle East democratic. The idea was that just as Latin America had turned away from military dictatorships during the previous decade, it was now time to refashion the Middle East. It did not quite work out, and the American occupation of Iraq made a mess of its transition from dictatorship to democracy. But it did eventually make Iraq a sort of democracy. Iraq is the only Arab country which has a Shi'a majority. This majority had been oppressed for centuries by Sunni rulers, including Saddam towards the end. Now that Iraq is a democracy, the Shi'a majority is asserting itself and sectarian quarrels continue.

The defeated Taliban and Al Qaeda did not disappear. In the mayhem following Saddam's removal, there were new formations. The Kurds wanted their own territory of Kurdistan and have established an independent military presence. The territory they covet lies in three neighbouring countries—Syria, Iraq and Turkey. The stragglers of Al Qaeda and other jihadi groups have now come together as Islamic State of Iraq and Syria (ISIS) or Daesh under a new self-styled caliph, Abu Bakr al-Baghdadi. By taking the name of the first of the caliphs, Ibrahim Awwad Ibrahim al-Badri is appealing to the long-dormant longing for a caliph among Sunni Muslims. He has no qualifications to be a caliph. All previous caliphs have claimed some connection with the Prophet or his tribe, the Quraysh. Even so, the very existence of a caliph has its resonance among Sunni Muslims. The appeal of this gesture is hard for non-Muslims to appreciate. The West sees him as a terrorist, but even when he is defeated or dead, the appeal of the caliphate will remain.

The most recent chapter in the Middle East is the war in Syria. Syria is a Shi'ite regime in a Sunni-majority country. The rebellion is against Bashar al-Assad, who has inherited the presidency from his father. But he has not been a democratic ruler. The rebellion against him has got mixed up with the jihadi groups also fighting for territory. Shi'a jihadi groups, such as Hezbollah in Lebanon, are ready to help Assad. Iran is also willing to come to the help of its fellow Shi'a ruler, even as the Sunni Kingdom of Saudi Arabia is willing to help the rebels.

The Syrian war has not ended (as of August 2017). Millions have been made refugees and live in Jordan and Lebanon. Aleppo has been razed to the ground with the UN helplessly trying its best to rescue civilians; if only Syria and its partner-in-crime Russia would relent. Some chance! Thousands have moved to Europe, and many more aspire to. This has led to considerable tension among the countries of the EU.

The Syrian war has been further complicated by Russia coming to the aid of Assad. Vladimir Putin, the Russian leader, has given military support to Syria. It is said that he wants access to a salt water port on the Mediterranean in return for that help. Putin has been aggressive in seizing Crimea and occupying Eastern Ukraine. This has led to sanctions against him by NATO countries. This has made the negotiations for cessation of the Syrian war difficult. The Western nations want Assad out and the rebel groups in power. Russia's presence complicates this situation as does the fact that some of the Islamist groups of Al Qaeda and ISIS are also involved in the war.

The arrival of Donald Trump has added a new element to this problem. Even within his first hundred days, Trump revealed himself as a unilateralist when it comes to foreign affairs. He did not consult NATO or the Allies. He reacted to the news that Syria had used chemical weapons on its citizens killing many children by dropping the largest non-nuclear bomb in America's arsenal. He had been suspected of collusion with Putin in the days before his inauguration, but now no one knows which way he will react in Syria.

Challenge to Tolerance

It is very difficult for anyone in the LO, or indeed anyone who is reconciled to modernity, to appreciate the fanaticism of the religious terrorist. The presence and persistence of the jihadi more or less since the beginning of the triumph of the West over USSR has been a formidable challenge to the values of liberal societies. This challenge has centred on the issue of integration of Muslims into Western societies where they have arrived in large numbers often from former colonies. Across Europe, nations have faced the challenge of reconciling the right of any community to follow the rules of its own culture while integrating with their new home environment which espouses the values of human rights and equality. It has led to clashes about the dress of Muslim women—the hijab and the niqab. The hidden face behind the veil makes the liberal uneasy and s/he suspects oppression of the one who has to don these costumes. But on the other hand is the idea that people must be allowed the freedom to live their own lives in their own way.

France has recently banned the burkini, and Germany has objected to the niqab. Muslims, on the other hand, especially the religiously devout, believe that they have to reject the values of modernity if they are to live the good life as enjoined by the Koran. One could say that Europe was in this situation five hundred years ago, and wars of religion were as bloody in Europe as anywhere else. But it is not easy just to hope that history will repeat itself and Muslims will embrace modernity. That would be both arrogant and deluded. In any case, such change may take centuries. It does not help meet the present challenge.

The modern cosmopolitan person takes religion lightly, more as a cultural choice than deep belief. Of course, there are groups among us who do take religion seriously—Jehovah's Witnesses, Baptists, Mormons, the Amish and Orthodox Jews. We tolerate them whatever their beliefs because, let us face it, they are one of us. Islam remains a stranger. Its challenge to our tolerance lingers. There are also Hindus, Sikhs and Buddhists, but their strangeness intrudes less. They are also less hostile to modernity.

There has also been the issue of religious education in schools run by religious establishments and in general, about the suspicion that Muslims are easy fodder for terrorists. In Europe, the Dutch followed a very liberal policy of tolerance of the Muslim culture, but soon found that on issues like women's clothes, rights of homosexuals and secular education, there was no meeting of minds between Muslims and the local population. France was opposed to religious education or even wearing of religious ornaments by pupils in state-run schools—Laïcité being their proud banner. There have been difficulties about integration. How can one reconcile tolerance with a community which insists that a separate existence, that is, non-integration, is its chosen stance? UK has also faced the dilemma despite allowing religious schools and choice in dress. Germany decided it could not approve of Muslim women hiding their faces behind the chosen dress. There is a continuous battle between tolerance and integration.

But there is a greater difficulty regarding the militant jihadi movement. Islamism is a political urban guerrilla movement which sees itself as engaged in a perennial war with the West. The jihadis revive memories of the medieval Crusades. Their battle is unrelenting, and they claim religious sanction for it based on their reading of the Holy Koran. It is a sectarian and puritanical reading. But there has not been enough debate within the Muslim community about the validity of the Wahhabi reading of the Koran. It is often the Muslim youth in Western countries suffering from alienation who get recruited by the Islamists. Yet again, the limits of tolerance are tested.

There is a long history of Christian anti-Semitism. This came to a tragic climax in the Holocaust. Now the idea of a common Judaeo-Christian tradition has been carefully fostered. The enmity between Islam and the two earlier Abrahamic faiths goes back to before the start of the second millennium of the Common Era. Muhammad claimed that he had been chosen to tell the world that he was the last Prophet, and that God—Allah—was telling the world through him that mankind had wasted the two earlier messages (in the Old and New Testaments). He (Muhammad) represented the final chance for mankind to follow the correct path. Unlike the earlier prophets, he had been spoken to directly by God. Thus, Muslims believe that Islam superseded earlier Abrahamic religions.

Christians have never accepted this claim. Muslims overran Southern Europe and North Africa in the seventh and eighth centuries. They occupied the southern parts of Spain for seven centuries. Europeans tried to challenge the Muslim conquest of Jerusalem. The Crusades spanned centuries in the medieval ages, but ultimately the Muslim occupation did not end. The battles continued between the Ottoman Empire and the European rulers of Austria and Venice. It was only after the Battle of Lepanto in 1571 that the balance turned in favour of the Christians, when a league of Catholic kingdoms defeated the Ottoman Navy.

The Christian dislike of Islam could be quite strong. Reading Thomas Carlyle's essay on Muhammad as a great historical personality gives an insight into the popular prejudice against the Prophet and his message in the Victorian period. Nothing much has improved.*

---

*Thomas Carlyle. 1841. *On Heroes, Hero-Worship and the Heroic in History: Six Lectures*. London: J. Fraser.

There has been a long debate among Muslims about the challenge that modernity poses. Christianity went through a battle against modernity for over two hundred years. The modernists doubted the existence or even the necessity of a God. They treated the Bible like any other historical text and subjected it to a critical analysis. Jesus Christ was treated like any other human being rather than the chosen Son of God by the mid-nineteenth century when David Strauss wrote the first biography of Christ in 1835. Darwin's work on the origin of the species and the role of natural selection in establishing the evolution of human beings undermined the Biblical account of creation. The Church had to accommodate modernity, although even to this day, the Catholic Church has adapted to modernity less than the Protestant Church.*†

Islam has not faced these many challenges. The position of the Koran is unchallenged as the divine word as heard by Prophet Muhammad. The few critical studies of the Koran that exist are in obscure academic journals and texts. Indeed, in the last fifty years, mainly through Saudi Arabia, the position of the ultra-orthodox Wahhabi sect has been propagated as the only true version of Islam. This sect's views have informed the young jihadists. If anything, the distance between Islam and modernity has widened.

Terrorism has become an ever-present danger to modern life. Most of it comes from Islamist jihadis, but not all. The facile assumption is that all terrorists are Muslims (leading often to the logical fallacy of saying all Muslims are terrorists). Over the last two centuries, the face of the terrorist has changed. In the nineteenth

---

*Charles Darwin. 1859. *The Origin of Species*. Oxford: Oxford University Press.
†Charles Darwin. 1871. *The Descent of Man, and Selection in Relation to Sex*, Volume 1, 1st edition. London: John Murray. UK: John Murray.

century, it was the anarchists who were feared for their tendency to assassinate political leaders as they did with President McKinley and Czar Alexander II. Nationalists in many colonies resorted to terrorism to register their protest. Ireland, India, Egypt and many other colonies had nationalists who were denounced as terrorists. Then came the communists and the fascists. For the British, from 1968 to 1998, it was terrorism originating in the sectarian dispute in northern Ireland which was a constant danger. Sri Lanka has been through a twenty-five-year civil war from the 1980s onwards where Tamil freedom fighters battled the national army. Predominantly Hindu and long settled on the island, the Tamil rebels were fighting to establish their own separate nation. The Tamil Tigers, as they were called, invented the idea of a suicide bomber, using women and children for the dangerous act. Colombia has just settled its decade-old battle against a rebel guerrilla force within its borders. India has had rebellion from the Maoist Naxalites movement in the north-east border regions of Nagaland and during the 1980s in Punjab. It is important to remember these cases so as to avoid the notion that terrorism is a recent phenomenon or that it is an exclusively Muslim activity.

The LO has conveniently forgotten its imperialist past and struggles in distant lands can barely engage its attention. In that way, the LO is historically myopic or rather only remembers its own version of history. Thus, it regards terrorism by the Islamist jihadis as the principal if not the only fear.

USA was defeated in Vietnam by a guerrilla army, which defied the superior technology that the Americans could deploy, by using simple weapons, but avoiding a standard war of two armies facing each other. The guerrilla warrior melted into the countryside because he was fighting on his native ground. The Americans never developed a counter-guerrilla armed force. Today, the Islamist is using guerrilla tactics in crowded urban areas. The jihadi is also on familiar ground because two, if not three, generations of colonial diaspora have settled in the urban centres of Europe. It is a sort of home turf. It is not clear how long the war against terror would last, but its presence has challenged some assumptions about citizenship in a multicultural and multiracial tolerant world.

Things Fall Apart

Dialectics is a mode of thinking that is no longer taught or used. But one rule of dialectical thinking enjoins us to look for a weak spot in the strongest part of the structure we are confronting. That proved to be the case with the global financial system. The financial markets had grown enormously in terms of the value of transactions, the number of equity and bond markets, and the many innovations in the list of assets which could be traded—swaps, options and derivatives, for instance. Banks had become bigger and a shadow banking system had developed for investing your money—hedge funds, for example. It had become much easier than before for ordinary people to get debit and credit cards and to borrow money for daily purchases or get mortgages for house acquisitions.

The growth of markets from the mid-1970s onwards (after the abandonment of the gold–dollar link) had coincided with the academic economist's propagation of the idea that markets were efficient. Markets made the best use of all available information and could not be captured or manipulated. Economists also argued that people made decisions rationally with the full knowledge of the working of the markets. Thus, policymakers could not enforce behaviour which people found to be in conflict with rational construction of how things work.

Economists were proud that their subject, despite all the criticisms it received, had been the instrument for avoiding a repetition of a 1930s'-style depression. After much debate between Keynesians and Monetarists, it had been settled that the cause of inflation was a loose monetary policy. Excessive money creation had its root in government deficits, that is, loose fiscal policy. Thus, it was agreed that fiscal policy ought to maintain the discipline of balanced budgets or, at worst, moderate deficits. It was preferable that the government present a medium-term macroeconomic projection laying out its tax and spending policy. The control of money supply and the setting of interest rates had to be the responsibility of an independent central bank. Financial markets were supposed to be working efficiently so it was best to leave them with as few regulations as possible. The people who were active in the markets were to be left to assess the risks of their actions and to bear the consequences.

The long boom of the 1990s continued over into the new century. There was a short sharp shock when the dotcom boom triggered by the new products of information technology and communications collapsed at the turn of the century. But monetary policy was made accommodative to soften the impact. The boom resumed. Inflation being low, interest rates were low. New financial products were attracting more customers into the market.

One such product was the securitization of mortgages. The mortgage on a house was a well-known, old financial product. There was legislation during the Clinton presidency to extend housing loans to families which would normally not qualify—families with precarious incomes and no history of credit. These were called subprime mortgages. A way was found to bundle together many mortgages into a security and then cut it up into several small shares. Thus, for example, one could take a thousand mortgages of $100,000 and chop up the bundle of $100 million into ten thousand shares of $10,000 each. They would be bought by banks and insurance companies as investments with a predictable income stream.

Banks sold these securitized mortgage shares to each other. Each felt the risk was spread by sharing it across the sector. One could further issue derivatives against the movements of such assets or even the movements in their price index. A towering inverted pyramid was constructed from a base of cash to credit and then on to lending and securitized assets based on this lending.

Interest rates had been low for many years. USA was running a double deficit in its budget and trade account. The wars in Iraq and Afghanistan as well as the tax cuts that George W. Bush had delivered led to a lot of public spending and deficit. The economy was growing, but importing more than exporting. Economists had found a sound defence of this errant behaviour. Asian countries had learnt from their shock in 1997 that they had to save and build up their reserves. The world was thus suffering from excess savings in Asia. The American policymakers made a virtue of their profligacy and claimed that by becoming 'consumer of the last resort', USA was keeping the global economy strong.

But the Chinese economy was growing at breakneck speed exporting its products to the West, mainly USA. It consumed a lot of raw materials and energy which it had to import. This put pressure on prices. The inflation signal began to flash red. The Fed was obliged to hike interest rates. The mortgage market had thrived because of low interest rates. Otherwise, the subprime mortgages, many of which would be defaulted upon, would never have been profitable. So it was no surprise that the first victim of the hike in the interest rate was a mortgage issuer.

On 15 August 2007, the thirty-sixth anniversary of Nixon's speech which unilaterally reneged on America's gold commitment, Countrywide Financial, the largest mortgage issuer, found that it could not raise enough short-term loans to meet its liabilities. House prices had been rising for a while and many were borrowing to buy a house in the hope that rising price would allow them to sell and repay the mortgage. With rising interest rates, the house price bubble collapsed. Countrywide Financial could not get help from the Federal Reserve. It had to be bought out by the Bank of America.

The contagion spread. In September 2007, Northern Rock, an aggressive mortgage lender in London, went under when the rumour spread that it did not have enough cash to let the depositors withdraw their money. It had to be taken over by the UK government before a buyer could be found for it. Then, in March 2008, Bear Stearns, an investment bank of long standing, found itself in difficulty. It had assets of $400 billion, but debts of $33 per dollar of its capital. Its share price collapsed and it was sold to JP Morgan Chase for $10 per share, when not very long before its share price had been $133. Then insurance company AIG ran into trouble and had to be rescued by the US government despite all the stuff about free markets.

The Bush government began organizing a rescue operation despite its firm belief that markets should be left to themselves without government interference. The Troubled Assets Recovery Plan (TARP) put $800 billion of taxpayers' money to buy out distressed financial corporations. Profits were private, but losses were socialized and paid for by taxpayers.

The towering inverted pyramid of easy credit and bad investments crashed on 15 September 2008 when Lehman Brothers went bankrupt. Lehman was not a bank, but a financial intermediary which had claims against banks and vice versa. It went from a valuable company at $600 billion to nothing rapidly. The US Department of Treasury was not willing to rescue it. Business froze, and the market collapsed. Despite the confident boasts of economists, a recession, later to be called the Great Recession, began in 2008. Few could predict that it would cripple Western economies for the next many years.

The Great Recession was the first major setback to Western economies since the Great Depression before the war. Three generations had grown up without experiencing income loss or unemployment on this scale. There had been inflation and even stagflation. But this was different. It was not supposed to happen. The first reaction of economists and policymakers was the same as that of military generals and political leaders at the onset of the First World War. It will be a short engagement. Troops/jobs will be back by Christmas. The war lasted four years. The Great Recession has lasted twice as long. For those who had begun to lose out when the manufacturing industry began to move out in the mid-1970s after the oil shock, the situation was grim. They had soldiered on without their wages rising. They had been encouraged to borrow to spend on the never never. Now even that consolation was gone. These people, mainly the white working class in USA and elsewhere in Europe, were bitter.

The political system coped in its traditional way. The Keynesian message had been to cushion any rise in unemployment by giving benefits. Public spending had to be allowed to increase. Government debt rose as tax revenues had fallen. Budget deficits as percentage of GDP rose to double digits in many countries. There was a danger that debt servicing may get even more expensive as creditors sold the debt and took their money abroad to safer markets.

Again, there was an attempt to play by the old rules. Gordon Brown, the prime minister of UK, chaired a G20 meeting in London and appealed for all developed nations to get together and launch a coordinated spending boost. But the markets had changed. They were wary of any more public spending. The firm resolution at the London conference melted away when the political leaders went back home.

Queen Elizabeth asked the question on everyone's mind. While inaugurating a new economics department building at the London School of Economics, she asked the economists gathered, 'Why did nobody notice it?' She was told by the young professor who was showing her around that it was 'a failure of collective imagination of many bright people'.

What the new generation of economists did come up with was a cure based on the simple idea of not repeating mistakes made during the Great Depression. Ben Bernanke, who had become chairman of the Federal Reserve, had studied the Great Depression as a research student during his university years and examined the argument by Milton Friedman that the Fed had blundered by tightening monetary policy during the 1930s when it should have relaxed it. Bernanke thus proceeded to activate monetary policy by buying government bonds in the market. This was not new; it used to be called Open Market Operations. But the scale of the buying was unprecedented. It was designed to bring interest rates down. Quantitative Easing (QE), as it was called, soon became the policy of choice of UK as well.

The effectiveness of three or four years of bond purchases in combating the recession is still being debated. It is argued that things would have been worse if QE had not been undertaken. The main effect of QE has been to lower interest rates.* Many companies with debts to service as well as mortgage holders with flexible interest rate mortgages have gained. As bond yields fell, the sellers of bonds switched to equity whose price had gone up. One effect, therefore, has been to enrich bond holders and equity buyers.

The effect of QE on income has been muted. The US economy, like in the UK, took seven years for the level of GDP to regain the pre-recession level. This has thus been the longest post-war recession. Incomes, especially of wage and salary earners, have been stagnant or falling in real terms in USA and UK. Unemployment rose immediately after the Lehman shock, but has been back down since.

Barack Obama won the election in 2008. One of his first acts was to initiate an $800 billion recovery programme. But soon after, he faced a hostile Congress which refused to grant any further expansion in expenditure as deficits might rise. The US debt-to-GDP ratio also rose fast as tax revenues declined and public expenditures stayed constant or went up to pay unemployment benefits. The battle between Obama and the Congress had an added racist element to the normal antagonism of politics. Obama's presidency as the first black (or mixed race) incumbent led to the growth of the Tea Party Movement, which was virulently right wing and openly resentful of a

---

*Buying bonds raises their price and the return or the yield on the bond moves inversely to its price. Price rises, yield falls.

non-white occupant of the White House. Bipartisan consensus was broken for the last six of the eight years of the Obama presidency. Instead of increasing public spending, an automatic process of sequestration has been put into play. Fiscal policy has been absent as a cure for the recession.

The Crisis in the Eurozone

The euro had been inaugurated on 1 January 1999 after careful preparation of several years and was hailed as a great innovation. One motivation was to rein in the powerful German economy. Germany had a strong currency, the Deutschmark. With the fall of USSR, Germany had also reunited with much anxiety in France, UK and other countries which had fought it in the Second World War. The setting up of the Eurozone and Germany joining it, were the conditions for the rest of the Allies to approve of the reunification. The criteria for admission were strict, but there was a willingness to be flexible in admitting countries into the Eurozone.

All eleven currencies were merged into the euro with exchange rates fixed as of their market rates on the last day before the creation of the euro. The ECB was put in charge. It had evolved from many intermediate preparatory monetary institutions which had been monitoring the development towards a single currency.

The demise of the Soviet Union encouraged the EC to enlarge its membership by including the countries of Eastern Europe. They had to adopt the EC's corpus of laws and regulations—the *acquis communautaire*.

The first few years of the euro were very successful. The boom in the world economy and the free movement of capital helped the members of the Eurozone. Eurozone countries seemed a safe bet. But while the Eurozone was a single currency area, it was not a single economic area. Each member country was responsible for its own debt. During the initial months of the recession, the single currency area seemed a safe haven. But by 2009, it was clear that there were weaknesses. Greece had piled up a debt which it was finding hard to service and it was in a serious crisis. To qualify to join the Eurozone, it had distorted its national statistics. In 2008, when this news came out, the interest rate payable on its bonds went up sharply (bond prices collapsed). Its true budget deficit in 2008–09 turned out to be 15 per cent. Its debts were too large for it to pay back or service. It needed outside help. Had there been an overall fiscal authority in the EU collecting taxes and arranging transfer of resources from the centre to the units, it could have been relieved. It could not renege on its debts as the Eurozone discipline did not allow unilateral action of that kind. The creditors wanted their money back. Soon the contagion spread to other economies suspected of having borrowed too much. Spain had received a lot of private investment in its real estate market, Ireland had private banks which had unsustainable debts, Italy and Portugal also had problems. Soon, the acronym PIIGS (Portugal, Italy, Ireland, Greece and Spain) became the dominant term to denote problem countries of the Eurozone.

Greece needed outside help to manage its debt. The ECB, the EC and the IMF—the troika—pooled their expertise to help Greece. One solution was to persuade the private creditors to 'have a haircut', that is, agree that their debts will not be paid back fully and agree to a write down. Private creditors accepted a 50 per cent haircut. But the borrowings from Eurozone members (by virtue of unpaid trade deficits) could not be legally written down. The troika agreed to lend money to Greece to bail it out. But they insisted that Greece cut its public spending drastically. Politically, this was suicide for any ruling government to agree. Several governments fell, and many elections had to be held. Cutting government spending has meant massive unemployment—25 per cent and above. It has meant a prolonged depression. There have been several bailouts by now, but the economic chance of Greece living within its means within the Eurozone is scant. Even so, Greece has not exited the Eurozone. The depression has now lasted for eight years. A far-left party, Syriza, which had come to power promising not to accept the troika's conditions, has nevertheless accepted the inevitable once in power, and is administering austerity. There has also been the rise of a far-right fascist party in the process.

Other Eurozone countries in debt have managed their affairs better. It has required budget cuts and no borrowing. Unemployment has been often intolerably high. There has been a problem in southern European countries of tax evasion and corruption, which has made economic management difficult. Vested interests resist cuts in spending. The price has been paid by the younger generation which has faced continued unemployment for years, and the elderly who have found their pensions eroded.

Along the way, the traditional right and left mainstream parties have been crowded out by extremes on both sides. There is the left-wing party Podemos in Spain, the left anarchist Five Stars party in Italy and Syriza in Greece. Even in Germany, which is not in economic crisis, there is a new right-wing group, Alternative für Deutschland (AfD). In UK, the United Kingdom Independence Party (UKIP) has been effective in its anti-EU stance, though it has suffered a decline since its main demand for Brexit won in the referendum. In the local elections during May 2017, UKIP lost all but one of its 150 seats. In the general election in June 2017, it lost the one seat it had. While elsewhere in Europe fringe parties gained, in UK they lost. While in France during the presidential elections the principal established parties of the right and left were rejected, in UK the two main parties captured 83 per cent of the total vote, the highest since 1970.

The Reckoning

In many ways, the rise of new fringe parties in developed countries denotes dissatisfaction with the economic performance, and by implication, political institutions and culture which have failed. The argument that a free market, liberal economic policy with strict fiscal discipline and an anti-inflationary monetary policy was all that was needed to reap the advantages of economic progress has been found wanting. Nationalism has become one of the forces to oppose liberal internationalism. As a result, the EU, which is a standard bearer of liberal values, has been subject to many strains.

The congruence of economic difficulties with terrorist attacks has increased the feeling of being beleaguered. The attack in January 2015 on the French satirical magazine *Charlie Hebdo* as a retaliation by the Islamists for what they perceived to be a sacrilegious cartoon of the Prophet shocked the world. The liberals believe in freedom of speech and expression without restraint. The religious fanatic enforces what he sees as a just punishment for transgression against his religion. France has continued to suffer terrorist attacks in Paris and then, recently, in Marseilles. Belgium saw its airport attacked.

A bus drove through a Christmas crowd in Berlin in the final weeks of 2016. In late April 2017, days before the first round of the presidential elections, a policeman was shot dead by a terrorist on the busiest Champs-Élysées in Paris.

These attacks contrast vividly with the generous welcome the EU accorded to refugees from the Syrian war during 2015. Germany, under the leadership of Chancellor Angela Merkel, admitted a million refugees. Further arrivals of refugees have led to some serious disputes within the EU. But the liberal attitude towards refugees shows that there is yet a desire to maintain some high ideals. These ideals could be under threat. Whether they are or not, will be the theme of our subsequent argument.

TWO

OUTSIDERS IN POLITICS:
NARENDRA MODI AND DONALD TRUMP

Donald Trump's surprise victory has unleashed anger and despair among the liberals of many nations. The idea that a man with openly misogynistic, if not predatory tendencies, xenophobic and racist (towards Muslims and Mexicans), proud of his business dealings, which included not paying taxes (legitimately), can be elected the president of the most powerful democracy has shocked them. The LO spreads across countries and continents and covers some of the best print media, TV stations, blogs and online magazines. It is an international hegemonic project which has set the tone of what can and should be said and what is taboo for some fifty years now. These are the beautiful people, right thinking, tolerant, good and do-gooders, convinced of their entitlement to rule politically and culturally.

It was not meant to happen. Throughout his campaign in the primaries, Donald Trump broke all the rules of decorum and polite speech. He trashed his rivals and humiliated the media personnel. He insulted various people, including Senator John McCain, a senior Republican and a former presidential candidate as well as a Vietnam hero. He doubted McCain's bravery just as he cast aspersions on the impartiality of a judge of Mexican origin. He demonized Muslims and illegal Mexican immigrants. The Republican establishment despaired of him and wished for his downfall. But he still got nominated.

As the campaign proceeded, Trump targeted his rival Hillary Clinton in the rudest possible terms, saying she should be locked up and would be if he came to power. He was exposed in a tape, making injudicious comments about how he liked to sexually assault women. Following this revelation of the old tape, many women came forward to relate how he had harassed them or invaded their space. He looked certain to lose.

All the polls had already showed that he would lose. Hillary Clinton was universally projected by all pollsters to win easily. She had it in the bag. Most newspapers, including many traditionally Republican ones, endorsed her. Colin Powell, among other Republican grandees, said he would vote for Hillary Clinton. Barack and Michelle Obama came out to support her in the final days of the campaign. Everyone who mattered was sure Clinton would win. *The New York Review of Books*, in its 27 October–9 November 2016 edition, carried a lead article by Robert Darnton with the cover titled 'Hillary's Big Chance…with Books'. It was an article about libraries, especially the Library of Congress, and its new head Carla Hayden.

Hillary Clinton was expected to be in the White House with a role to play in encouraging libraries round the country.

Then, on 9 November 2016, Trump won more Electoral College votes than Clinton, while she won three million more votes than he did. It was thus a knife-edge decision. It was not a landslide by any means. It reflected a detailed unceasing strategy of getting the vote out till the last minute of the last hour before the polls closed in the crucial Midwestern states on the part of Trump's adviser Steve Bannon (since appointed chief strategist and denounced for allegedly being a white supremacist). Clinton's campaign was perhaps too complacent and too credulous of the opinion polls. She won big where she did and piled up the votes, but she did not win widely enough geographically. It has been calculated that the boroughs of New York, except Staten Island and LA County, account for more than her three million margin. Take that out and Trump has 500,000 more votes than Clinton. On the other hand, his victory margin in Wisconsin, Michigan and Pennsylvania was wafer-thin—less than 100,000 overall. Even so, the rules of the game say that you have to win those counties even if by one vote. By the end, the map of USA was blue at the edges and blood red in the middle, like an over-frozen haunch of beef.

Trump's victory was unexpected, unwelcome and, in many eyes, undeserved. The losers were angry, frightened for their country and in denial that this could happen. Sober analysts have tried to reach apocalyptic conclusions about the future of the LO and Western civilization, not to say the human race threatened by climate change upon the arrival of Trump.

There were demonstrations and marches through many cities of USA with people shouting 'Not my President'. They also carried placards declaring 'The Whole World is Watching', little aware that ironically the first time the sign was displayed was in 1968 when young people were protesting outside the Democratic Convention in Chicago. The enemy then was Lyndon Johnson and the Democratic Party. And indeed much of the world was watching the convention on TV (as I was). The villain this time was the other party and another president (elect).

Yet, it was a narrow victory, driven by the vagaries of the rules of the Electoral College, a device reflecting the suspicion in which the founding fathers held the popular vote. A simple count across the country would have given Clinton the job. But this would imply that the larger states could dominate USA. It was to guard against that possibility and the alienation it would cause in the smaller states that the founding fathers invented the Electoral College. What the vote says is that USA is a deeply divided nation along the lines of white and black, the educated college graduates and the undereducated high-school leavers, the rural versus the urban and the prosperous coastline states versus the depressed middle. And even then the turnout in this most bitterly fought election was only 57 per cent. Only half the nation voted and only a smaller half of that half chose Trump.

How come no one believed that Trump was electable? I was able to see it way back in April 2016. Here was a candidate who, by his unorthodox campaign and controversial personality, was able to break the rules of American electoral politics. Trump was a master of the TV medium, having been a presenter of many shows. He knew, more than any other politician, that the attention span of a viewer was short and the ways to create a controversy. Indeed, of all the presidential candidates of the post-1945 world, Trump knew the TV medium better than anyone else. His outrageous views led some people to conclude that he was stupid, but he knew precisely what he was doing. He got a lot of free publicity saying what he did and the way in which he did. Still, no one could see that he was an extremely effective campaigner.

The President in a British-style Cabinet System

In my blog in the online magazine *Globalist* (26 April 2016) titled 'Is Donald Trump the Narendra Modi of the USA?', I analysed the election of Narendra Modi as the head of the parliamentary campaign of the Bharatiya Janata Party (BJP) in the 2014 Indian general elections. He was a controversial figure who had been blamed for an extremely violent communal riot in February 2002 in which Hindus, the majority community in India, had allegedly attacked and killed many Muslims in the state of Gujarat (where Modi was the chief minister). It was the first riot filmed on 24x7 television channels, which had just arrived in India a few years previously. As a result, he had been denounced by human rights groups and refused visa to visit most Western democracies. I had denounced the riots of 2002, though blamed the majority community rather than the political leadership.*

India has a British-style system in which elections are held for the 545 seats in the Lok Sabha, the federal people's chamber and the Indian equivalent of the US House of Representatives. The party or coalition of parties which gets a majority gets to form the

---

*Meghnad Desai. 2002. 'Gujarat and Its Bhasmita', Seminar in May 2002. Reprinted in: Meghnad Desai. 2005. *Development and Nationhood: Essays in the Political Economy of South Asia*. UK: Oxford, pp. 264–66.

government. There had been no single-party majority since 1989, but coalition governments and/or minority governments ruling with 'outside' support. In 2014, few expected that any party could get a majority on its own. The Congress party, which had ruled since independence in 1947 in 55 out of the 67 years, had just finished two terms as the leading party in a ruling coalition, the United Progressive Alliance (UPA). But it was losing popularity. The BJP had ruled at the head of a coalition National Democratic Alliance (NDA) in 1998–2004, but then it only had 181 seats instead of the 273 needed for a majority.

It looked unlikely that the BJP could make it, especially if it had chosen the controversial Narendra Modi as its lead candidate and hence the choice to be prime minister if they won a majority. Even the seniors within his party (much as the Republican grandees and Donald Trump) did not think he could win big. Indeed, they were hoping he would not. Then, he could be reined in by coalition partners. This was to allay their worry that Modi may prove less than even-handed when it came to the treatment of Muslims as against Hindus. This is labelled as communalism in India, which worries the country as much as racism worries the Americans. The Indian Constitution affirms the value of secularism—the even-handed treatment of all religious communities whether Hindus, Muslims, Christians, Sikhs or Parsees. They also feared that Modi would be authoritarian. The LO favoured the Congress party to win as it had secular credentials and many years' experience of wielding power.

I had been tracking the election as I had done earlier. I had followed Narendra Modi's career as the chief minister as he won successive elections in Gujarat in 2002, 2007 and 2012. State elections in India follow a different calendar cycle compared to the federal election. In December 2007, after the election results, I was asked on live television by Barkha Dutt, the then leading TV personality of the NDTV channel in New Delhi, what I made of Modi's victory. I was in Goa then taking part in the live telecast via a feed-in. I said, 'Narendra Modi is the next leader of the BJP.' This provoked surprise and some disgust because the idea of Modi going on to the national stage was unthinkable. Ashis Nandy, my friend and an internationally renowned psychologist and social scientist, who was on the same panel sitting in Delhi, said in response to my prediction, 'Over my dead body!' I replied, 'Ashis, you and I are young enough and it will happen in our lifetime.'

Monitoring Indian politics for my weekly column 'Out of My Mind' in *The Indian EXPRESS* every Sunday, I was able to plot the fragility of the Congress. They had just over 200 seats in the outgoing Parliament in 2014. I first predicted a loss of a hundred seats, then got round to a calculation that the Congress would get seats in double digits. I also raised my forecast of the BJP seats. On the day of the count, I was on the Times Now channel's election broadcast chaired by Arnab Goswami with his inimitable panache. We were a panel of journalists and political observers. In the pool, I bet as many as 265 seats, the most anyone had predicted. I was short of the final result by about 20 seats. But I won the pool as being closest to the final result. The BJP had secured a majority and Modi would be the prime minister.

The reaction in India was very similar to what has happened in USA with Trump. There was fear and incredulity. Through the campaign, all the leading print media had downplayed the chances of the BJP. Modi was seen as a flawed candidate for leadership. But he ran a vigorous, almost presidential, nationwide campaign with a powerful message of inclusive development. Most liberals refused to hear what he had to say and stuck to their view of him as a communalist politician. As Dileep Padgaonkar, a distinguished Indian journalist, said in his article, 'A Missive to Distraught Liberals', in *The Times of India* on 30 May 2014:

> We reckoned that BJP-led NDA would fail to reach the halfway mark. This would compel it to rope in 'secular' non-Congress, non-Left regional parties to take a shot at governance. The latter, we took it for granted, would extract their pound of flesh—deny Narendra Modi any role in the new dispensation. Towards this goal we added our two-penny bit. We missed no chance to harp on Modi's RSS background. Time and again, we raked up the 2002 violence in Gujarat.*

Modi won because he had a message which carried to the new voters who were children when the riots had taken place. They did not read newspapers but relied on social media. Modi had mastered the social media technology. He used Twitter imaginatively, made himself accessible online with a campaign team ever ready to respond to queries. This was the new technology of campaigning which the other parties were slow to replicate. Rahul Gandhi, the leader of the Congress party and the son, grandson and great-grandson of prime ministers, was younger than Modi but had no penchant for social media. Rather like Clinton, the Congress and Rahul Gandhi had a sense of entitlement. Power rightfully and due to historical primacy belonged to him. Modi was an interloper. There was also a caste hierarchy point. Rahul Gandhi and Congress leadership are

---

*http://blogs.timesofindia.indiatimes.com/talking-terms/a-missive-to-distraught-liberals/, accessed 9 June 2017.

upper caste, many are Brahmins. Narendra Modi is from a caste of oil-crushers, an Other Backward Caste (OBC) person. His father ran a tea-stall. Modi was thus a 'chai-wala' (tea-seller). As one Congress grandee said on TV, 'He will never be prime minister, but if he wants to come to our gathering and make tea, he can do so.'

Trump and Modi are both outsiders. They have a toxic image in the eyes of the liberal media. They are denounced as racist/communalist. Modi has never displayed misogyny though he is single, having abandoned his wife without consummating their teenage marriage. Modi has fashioned his life since his teenage days on the Indian (Hindu) ideal of renunciation and has dedicated his life to a higher cause. He wanted to follow the example of his namesake Narendranath Datta, who later became Swami Vivekananda. Vivekananda travelled to USA and spoke at the 1893 Parliament of the World's Religion in Chicago and spread the message of Hinduism around the world. Modi wanted to be an ascetic, but was advised to follow a worldlier path by the Ramakrishna Mission, named after the guru of Vivekananda. He joined the Rashtriya Swayamsevak Sangh (RSS), a social volunteer organization founded in 1925, which has a Hindu ideological orientation and works for national uplift. It has the image of an extreme right-wing organization, though it is not a political party. It has, however, survived for ninety years. Founded in the same year as the Communist Party of India, it has also outstripped the latter in effectiveness. Modi learnt the discipline of selfless service and frugal living in the RSS. He worked as a pracharak (carrier of the message). While he was doing unpaid volunteer political work, he also pursued his education and obtained his degree via correspondence course.

The RSS is the ideological mentor of the BJP. In 2002, Modi

who was until then in the RSS, was told to go to Gujarat where the BJP government was in some disarray. There had been an earthquake in Kutch, a part of Gujarat, and relief work was not up to the scratch. He was made the chief minister of Gujarat, his first political assignment. He started at the top. He still had to be elected to the legislative assembly.* He had been the chief minister barely six months when riots broke out.

Thus, Modi is less of an outsider in political terms, but more in social terms as they are defined in India. The elite is upper caste, anglophone and anglicized. Modi speaks in Hindi, as his first choice, though he can speak in English and has mastered it much more since he became the prime minister and began to travel abroad extensively. He also has experience as a chief executive officer (CEO), which is what a chief minister is. Thus, he arrived at the top with a background. He became the prime minister at the same time as he became a member of Parliament (MP). Unlike previous prime ministers of India, he was not familiar with the Delhi political scene. He has shown a tremendous capacity for hard work and has been effective in consolidating the position of the BJP as a ruling party across the different regions of India in the three years as the prime minister. Modi has been presidential in a British-style cabinet system.

Donald Trump and the New Rules of Politics

Trump, on the other hand, is very much a man of the world and always has been. Joining his father's business, he prospered by deal making and built a large empire of real estate, casinos and golf

---

*There is a six-month period within which a chief minister has to get elected.

courses. He has been married thrice and presides over a large family of children and their spouses and grandchildren. He is the richest person to be elected president. He is a self-publicist, making cameo appearances in movies and hosting TV shows. He is obviously very pleased with himself. The puzzle is that his achievements were under-appreciated. The mere fact that he was an outsider in party politics made the media treat him like a bumbling amateur, little realizing that Trump had smartly surveyed the existing practices in electoral politics and chosen not to tread the familiar path.

Donald Trump's victory on the iconic/ironic date 11/9 surprised everyone and shocked many. The establishment across the two parties in USA shunned and reviled him. They were incredulous that his manner of campaigning, of breaking every rule in their books, could win votes. He flaunted his money, his ego and his prejudices. He behaved true to himself. A politician with ambitions for higher office is not meant to do that. S/he has to separate the public persona and the private one, as Hillary Clinton confessed to doing. Professional politicians are house-trained, packaged, homogenized and have to learn to behave like a ventriloquist's dummy as manipulated by their experts, staffers and inner office.

As of now, there is anger among the young for whom this is the first experience of alienation from the political system. A previous younger generation—one which got labelled the Hippie generation—was alienated from American politics and society. It was the first time in decades that the elders were bewildered by the behaviour of the young. The 1960s saw a bitterly divided nation with a civil rights movement, the Vietnam War and the ideological shift rightwards, which brought Nixon and later Reagan to power. We could, once again, be looking at an age divide or a regional divide within the majority white community in America. It could even be that the young would have voted more assiduously than they did had they known Trump may win.

Even so, explanations and self-examination are required by those who had blithely assumed and predicted that Hillary Clinton would walk it. Pollsters, opinion makers and editorialists were near unanimous that Trump had no chance. He was something odious the cat had brought in. He would be dumped by the great American public. The near certainties of the predictions were faux scientific, but no one was in a mood to question.

During the campaign, Hillary Clinton labelled Trump supporters as deplorable, a collection of racists, xenophobes and misogynists. What was true is that Trump was appealing to groups who had felt excluded from the political process. Candidates in previous elections of either party spoke a similar language, and it was not the language of the people who felt ignored. The bipartisan consensus was marginally different as between the Republicans and Democrats. These small differences had to be exaggerated. As in normal business competition when two companies are selling a similar product, a lot of money has to be spent differentiating between what is the same. This is why it gets expensive. Elections have become massively exorbitant, requiring a lot of money to be raised, putting the winning candidate in thrall of the fund givers. Trump did not need to raise much money. A lot of Republican donors went to Clinton as they could not abide by Trump. At one late stage, someone even complimented Hillary Clinton as representing the Nelson Rockefeller wing of the Republican Party which had been marginalized by the Goldwater–Reagan–Bush party. She represented the amalgam of both parties which had become identical twins.

Trump escaped this trap. He went away from centrist politics with its polite discourse. He was not house-trained as a professional politician. He looked out for and garnered the vote banks previously ignored. This vote bank is labelled white working class (though it seems to include only men as white; women are listed separately). They are also undereducated. This vote bank voted solidly for Trump, especially in the crucial Midwestern states. But white women are also undereducated and should be included in this vote bank. More of them voted for Trump than for Clinton.

The analysis as to why this group is deprived has been quite superficial. They are said to be the losers from globalization. But the phenomenon of globalization is dated as from the 1990s. The North American Free Trade Agreement (NAFTA) is blamed as is the rise of China. But the actual course of the economic deprivation of the white working class is longer and has different origins. The deindustrialization of Western economies was a phenomenon which began in the mid-1970s and has been in progress for forty years now in America, as we saw in the previous chapter. This has led to wages of ordinary manual workers being flat for those forty years.

This can be seen in average hourly earnings of production and non-supervisory workers. These figures are adjusted for consumer price inflation, and are what we call real wages. They peaked at just above $22 in the early 1970s. Then they declined to $18 during Clinton's first term and came up to under $21 in 2015. The share of wages and salaries in GDP had fallen from 50 per cent to 42.5 per cent over the same period. Yet total income had risen by three-and-a-half times between 1971 and 2015.

This downward course for workers' real wages for forty years has not been a burning question for economists or politicians in

USA. This scandalous fact has caused no shock to the American political system. The economic debate has traversed various themes of monetarism and the control of inflation, the Laffer curve and tax cuts, supply-side economics and then the Great Moderation, but no one has made the real wage decline a burning question of national politics. The worry among policymakers, for example at the Federal Reserve, has been the inflation–unemployment trade-off. Those numbers include the sectors where incomes are rising. Measures of employment indicate full employment, but the wage—average compensation of manual workers—is much lower than it used to be.

Those who have been at the short end of this saga have been frustrated. American ideology is of self-help and doing your best. But the system has not equipped the losers with enough education to escape their predicament. No government has set aside money for re-skilling or brought industry to these regions. A firm belief in free markets has meant that things must take their course. Since the 1970s, America has turned itself from a manufacturing to a service economy. Thanks to Silicon Valley, there are flourishing service industries. The financial sector has expanded. What remains of manufacturing is high skill, advanced technology industries such as aerospace and pharmaceuticals. Incomes in the higher echelons are rising. There are high rewards in higher education. But beneath the prosperous metropolitan America of the East and West Coasts is the depressed middle, the country that one flies over. Here are families in which both adults need to work sometimes in more than one job. Their children cannot afford to go beyond school and so join the poverty league of their parents.

Helplessness in a culture which prizes individual effort and enterprise fuels resentment. You need to blame someone for your plight. Politics and politicians who make tall promises but do not deliver or who plead helplessness due to external constraints are prime candidates for blame. Tax cuts for the rich are all right, but no help for the poor. The poor are too proud to live on welfare which is meagre in any case. They resent Washington which stands for everything they believe is keeping them down. Their politics is anti-politics.

The white working class is not the only poor section. There are Black American families in a similar situation. They did not even have the thirty years of good wages which the white families enjoyed. Among the Black Americans, education has opened up an even sharper income divide than among the white. But even so, there is no feeling of solidarity between the poor White and poor Black Americans. If anything, the penurious white worker blames the black worker as having enjoyed civil rights and muscled in on his job, as 'line-cutter' or queue jumper, as the British would say. Not true, but resentment does not have logic. No political party has galvanized this anger of the poor black and white workers. If anything, the antagonism still festers and is allowed to.

The schism between the white and black deprived sections became sharper with the Obama presidency. Many white workers in the midwest had voted for Obama in the 2008 elections. But as the effects of the 2008 crisis began to hurt, Washington, and now a black president, were once again blamed. Even after fifty years of civil rights legislation, the election of a black (strictly speaking mixed race) president stirred some deep sense of entitlement among the white. This is because the acceptance of equal rights legislation had good middle-class support, and many black people had been able to benefit and join the middle class. But what the better-off did not mind was not acceptable at the lower end of the income level.

There was also the birth of the Tea Party Movement coinciding with the Obama presidency. Actually, the roots of the Tea Party go back to the early 1960s with the John Birch Society and Barry Goldwater's nomination as the presidential candidate in 1964. After the bipartisan consensus of the 1950s, sharp left–right differences (less sharp than in Europe, of course) began to appear. Various right-wing sects—libertarian, populist, conservative and constitutionalist—began to grow. William Buckley Jr was the sophisticated end of this upsurge. Barry Goldwater did not register a large vote, but his effort bore fruit with the election of President Ronald Reagan in 1980.

When he got elected as the first Democrat president since Jimmy Carter, Bill Clinton soon realized that the drift of American public opinion was rightward. Indeed, the global climate was that way. Clinton reformed the welfare state to cut its size and followed orthodox fiscal rules (registering a rare instance of a budget surplus) and deregulated financial markets. All parties were of one ideology with only marginal differences.

It was the radical 'loony' right which held out against this homogenization of political ideology. America has no left-wing politics to speak of. The Tea Party argued for a smaller government, lower taxes and no foreign aid. Some were even against foreign interventions. They have a highly conservative or 'originalist' view of the constitution. They are against relaxing rules on abortion and gay marriage. They insist on the Second Amendment and the right to carry guns. They are as much trouble within the Republican Party as they were for the Democrats. They loathe Obamacare as an example of government interference with the free market in healthcare.

It is these forces and movements which the Republican Party ignored in 2008 and 2012, which Trump has accommodated. He does not share the fiscal orthodoxy of the Tea Party. He likes public debt and will borrow more while they abhor it. He shares their hatred of Washington and will 'drain the swamp' as soon as he can. What appealed to the white working class was not just Trump's dislikes, but his positive programme of job creation and infrastructure building.

Donald Trump represents the long march of the unfashionable right, but he has come from outside. The Republican Party has been unwilling to fully own up to these 'loony' right members. In UK, the Conservative Party treated the right-wing extreme party UKIP with similar contempt. Yet, when the referendum took place on staying or leaving the EU, it was the anti-EU faction of the Conservative Party which joined UKIP to win the referendum for Brexit. Trump has, in fact, leveraged the implicit divide in the Republican Party to win the presidency. The mainstream Republican politician, even when he secretly may have been of a Tea Party mode, felt compelled to hide it and move to the middle ground. Trump stayed on the fringe. He did not openly endorse the Tea Party, but he saw the empty spaces on the edges which the centrist politicians had ignored.

There is a broader issue of income inequality. This has become a fashionable topic among the LO. Thomas Piketty's book *Capital in the Twenty-First Century* (2014) has made people aware that the top 1 per cent has had huge increases in income compared to the rest. In terms of deciles, the top decile has also gained at the cost of the rest. But it is the Real Median Household Income (RMHI), the midpoint of the income distribution which is more revealing. It was in 1998 that the RMHI peaked at $58,000. By 2015, it had declined to $54,000.

Trump did not take up the generally fashionable issue of inequality either in terms of the top 1 per cent or the median income. He concentrated on the loss suffered by traditional manufacturing workers. The fashionable discussion dealt in the abstract in terms of the top 1 per cent or the top 10 per cent. Trump, like a shrewd politician, focused on a specific group who self-identified as working class and talked about their misery. He did not speak in terms of a progressive income tax, even of a global income tax as has been the case in the LO. He stuck to the specifics of job creation. He has even talked about bringing the old industries back. This has sent alarm bells ringing since it smacks of economic nationalism.

It was possible from a distance to see more clearly that Trump was doing many things right. Once you granted that he was a successful businessman, you could see that there was a shrewd plan behind his campaign. So why did the experts get it so wrong?

Conventional Wisdom

John Kenneth Galbraith, the Harvard political economist, invented the expression 'conventional wisdom'. This is something which sounds so plausible that after a while everyone stops questioning it. People who may not know where the idea originated acquire a sense of being in the mainstream by repeating what everyone else is saying.

One such conventional wisdom is that political parties should move to the centre as most voters are there. On the extremes, there are a few stragglers, but parties who cultivate them never get anywhere. The idea originates not in politics, but in location theory. In a classic paper in the early 1930s, Columbia professor and renowned statistician Harold Hotelling applied the idea to where shops should locate. Common sense would say locate your shop far away from your competitors so shops would be randomly distributed over a large space. But what if buyers were normally distributed over the same space? It would pay shops to be near each other, close to the buyers. If the distribution of buyers is bell-shaped, the centre (the mode) is where most buyers will be. So shops will hug together, competing for a common clientele visiting the market.

Anthony Downs developed this idea in his book *An Economic Theory of Democracy*. This idea is a non-ideological theory of democratic politics. Don't take your political philosophy and try to convince the voters. Find out what they want and package your policy to maximize votes. The Europeans were appalled as they liked ideology, but the Americans were thrilled. Just then, in the late 1950s, statistical tools and techniques were being developed. Voters could be surveyed about their preferences about policies. You could break down voters by class, race, gender, location, income and get an increasingly sophisticated predictor of voting behaviour.

As computers got faster and statistical techniques got more sophisticated, more data could be handled and analysed. Marketing and polling share the same goal. Each tries to gauge the market share of the product they want to sell. You inquire into the tastes of buyers and as they may be similar, try and locate tiny differences between them and train your appeal to heighten the idea that the product you are selling meets the desires of the buyer. The secret is not to deviate too far from the middle. Your toothpaste has to be the same as the others, but with a slight difference, which you hope will catch the buyer's fancy.

All this is prefatory to saying that Donald Trump ignored this theory. Instead of moving to the centre, he stayed on the extremes. He puzzled his rivals by his behaviour. During the primaries, his Republican rivals could not take him seriously. He was rude and insulting to candidates like Jeb Bush (a centrist par excellence) and Marco Rubio. No one thought he could be ahead at the end, but he was. The Democrats could not believe that a man whose speeches were racist, misogynist and macho had any chance of defeating a serious professional politician like Hillary Clinton who has the correct combination of liberal tolerant beliefs.

Now that Donald Trump has won, there will have to be a new way of modelling politics. Pollsters will have to stop asking the standard anodyne questions. They may have to find techniques where voters reveal their true preferences. This is not easy, as economic theorists have found out. Polling companies may also need to recruit pollsters from outside conventional wisdom clubs.

In the last three years, there have been three major reversals for pollsters. The 2014 Indian election surprised people because they shut their eyes and ears to what was happening. They kept on disbelieving that Modi could be taken seriously. The centre ground they were exploring no longer attracted the voters. Even his own party did not understand how he could win by breaking the rules.

To quote Dileep Padgaonkar, whom I quoted briefly earlier from his article in *The Times of India* of 30 May 2014:

> An equally miserable failure of ours was to underestimate the spell Modi cast on the electorate. Armed with a high-tech media blitz, he led an intensive, spirited campaign built around his personality. He tapped into voters' dismay and frustration over the ineptitude and shenanigans of the Manmohan Singh

dispensation. He pinned responsibility on Gandhi family's dynastic rule. He also tapped into voters' yearning for a leader endowed with the will and aptitude to bring prosperity to the people, ensure lean and effective governance, provide security and instil national pride in citizens.

The analysts in India were looking for the same old model of appealing to secularism and *Garibi Hatao* (Remove Poverty) type election message. That was the brand which had succeeded. Modi was away from that model. He fashioned a new brand which appealed to the voters precisely because it was not the same old message. This fooled the politicians and the pollsters.

The next two episodes were in UK. The Scottish Referendum on independence was misread by YouGov, a leading pollster. They predicted the independence vote to win on the eve of the vote. Panic ensued and David Cameron, the prime minister, and Gordon Brown, the former prime minister with his base in Scotland, made promises which would blunt the appeal of those who wanted independence for Scotland. The results, when they came, had a margin of 10 per cent points for the stay vote. The pre-vote panic was misplaced.

Then Brexit happened last June. Again, there was incredulity that the 'Out' vote could win. All the 'right-thinking' people knew it would be a disaster, and, hence people, would be sensible. What that meant was that people would think like them. The results showed a 4 per cent point margin in favour of 'Out'. Of the 34 million votes cast (nearly 75 per cent turnout), 18 million were for 'Out' and 16 million for 'Remain'. But in England, the margin was wider—7 per cent points—15 million for 'Out' and 13 million for 'Remain'. Pollsters were used to looking at Scotland or Wales separately as a region. But England, the overwhelmingly larger region, was never analysed on its own. As the results show, the margin of two million votes in England was also the national margin. That means the other three regions cancelled each other out.

The old Downs model is broken and cannot be fixed. That, if true, has a profound consequence for American politics. Instead of two large parties with similar profiles, we may get sharp ideological fractions which will not bid for majority but for a seat at the top in some coalition. Imagine if Bernie Sanders and Marco Rubio (or Jeb Bush) had also run. The outcome could have been such that the final result would have been thrown into the Congress than made by the Electoral College. European politics has been going this way since the Eurozone crisis.

The issue in centrist politics is to exaggerate small differences between the two parties. There is also a Manichean tendency to characterize the other as incredibly distant and unacceptable. But then, ex-post facto, there needs to be bipartisan cooperation to get things done. A series of developments in recent years has informed us that perhaps the electorate is not happy with the limited choice they are being offered. They want a change in the way politics is done. Their demands are not being heard by the establishment politicians. That is a serious problem the LO has to tackle.

THREE

MODI AND TRUMP AT WORK

On 8 November 2016, two events took place across the world. Americans were going to the polls to choose between Donald Trump and Hillary Clinton. At 20:00 hours Indian Standard Time (11:30 EST USA) far away in New Delhi, Narendra Modi took to the TV channels to make a major announcement. The speech had been flagged already. There was a tense atmosphere between India and Pakistan with cross-border skirmishes. It had been announced that Modi had met the chiefs of the Armed Services earlier in the day. Indians were expecting a major escalation of the conflict. Given that both the countries have nuclear capability, a conflict between the two is always fraught with danger.

In the event, Modi launched a bomb of a very different sort. He announced that as of midnight, higher denomination notes—₹1,000 (about $15) and ₹500—were demonetized. The citizens could bring them to be put in their bank accounts until December 31. In the meantime, the higher denomination notes would be accepted only for certain limited transactions—at railway stations, petrol pumps or for air travel, etc. New currency notes were to be issued for ₹500, and a new denomination note of ₹2,000 would also be introduced. He warned the listeners that there would be some hardship to follow. But he asked for their forbearance as this was necessary to combat corruption and illegal money transactions.

This sudden policy move, which became known as demonetization (though remonetization would have been a better choice), shook the country. It was not unusual. In January 1978, higher denomination notes of ₹10,000, ₹5,000 and ₹1,000 had been withdrawn and declared illegal. A similar operation had taken place in 1946 previously.

The devalorization of higher denomination notes was another stage of a fight against corruption which Modi has made a major plank of his government. The Indian economy has an elaborate tax system. Income tax is levied but being a poor country, only a small part of the population comes within its net. But given the large informal economy and with cash being the principal form of payment (estimated at 78 per cent of all transactions), a lot of money escapes income tax. The money that evades tax is called black money. Black money circulates in activities such as real-estate purchase, gold and jewellery, drug and prostitution. People who wish to buy property legally are told to get a percentage of the price in black money, paying the remainder legally. Black money generates profits which add to its volume. The size of the black economy in India has been a subject of much speculation. All measurements are speculative, but estimates have been roughly around a third to two-thirds of the official GDP.

All governments have been aware of this phenomenon. They have tried to entice black money back by offering amnesty from payment of the evaded tax or offered concessions by promising a lighter tax cut. A lot of money has also escaped abroad and is in foreign banks. Modi has been passionate about bringing this money back and uncovering black money. Estimates of the money abroad have been so inflated that he rashly promised that by bringing the money back he could give ₹1,500,000 to each and every citizen. This was based on an estimate by one of the economic think tanks of the RSS/BJP. Modi should have never taken the estimate seriously. For a population of 1.25 billion, it comes to ₹1.875 trillion. That much money could never have been exported abroad. Even if that were the case, the only amount the government could have confiscated would have been the tax unpaid plus a fine. The rest of the money would have remained the private property of the depositor and the Constitution guarantees the right to private property.

The announcement on 8 November was much more effective. As much as 86.9 per cent of all cash was in the two higher denomination notes, a value of ₹15.4 trillion. The withdrawal of the cash and its conversion into bank deposits was a sudden and total surprise. At the same time, the induction of new cash in the form of the high denomination notes of ₹500 and ₹2,000 was not as smooth as should have been the case. The ATM machines were unable to dispense the new notes as the ₹2,000 was of a new smaller size than the old ₹1,000 notes. The machines needed to be recalibrated.

There were long queues at banks and many tales of hardships for small traders, who did their business in cash, started coming through. Workers who got hired on a casual daily basis found that they could not be hired due to lack of cash. Lower denomination notes of ₹100 and below were at a premium. Older people who were used to keeping moderately large sums of money in cash at home were confused as to what would happen to their money.

Modi's opponents were in cock-a-hoop. After 900-plus days of his term in office, he seemed to have made a move that was very negative. People were being made to queue and had become fearful of what would happen. Soon, some opposition leaders were demanding an immediate withdrawal of the order. Prominent public figures, including an internationally renowned economist, doubted the legality of the move. He was wrong. It was compatible with the Reserve Bank of India (RBI) Act. Rahul Gandhi, the Congress vice president, said Modi had firebombed the poor. Dr Manmohan Singh, the previous prime minister, speaking in Parliament, predicted that GDP growth would fall by 2 per cent from its predicted value of 7.5 per cent. The Lok Sabha, the lower house of Parliament, was disrupted and had to be repeatedly adjourned by the speaker as was the Rajya Sabha.

Modi had done something big and radical. It could be a game changer, but it looked to many like he had made a blunder. Whatever the merits of the move, his behaviour was presidential as had been the case since 16 May 2014 when he had won the majority in the Lok Sabha. For a British-style system with the prime minister at the head of a cabinet and with constant interaction with Parliament, the usual model is collective responsibility with the prime minister as a consensual chairman. Modi has been different. He has handled his majority in such a way that he is the supreme leader. All the members of his cabinet are in awe of him. He is *primus inter pares*.

Modi's victory in 2014 had been a surprise and to the old liberal power brokers a shock. They could not believe that the BJP could win, especially if Modi was the lead candidate. Even less did they expect that he would be a successful prime minister. Modi had hit the ground running. He had the slogan of *Sabka Saath, Sabka Vikas* (All Together, Development for All) which signalled an inclusive development message. As he was widely suspected of being anti-Muslim, the inclusive part of his message was much doubted by his opponents.

Modi had shown that he had thought deeply about India's flagging growth performance as well as about the need to look after groups who had been left behind. Thus, he made the Dalits, formerly untouchables, a special focus of his development policies by establishing a special bank to help Dalit entrepreneurs. He also went beyond the narrow economic agenda to address wider issues which made India backward. He made cleanliness across the country a big campaign—Swachh Bharat Abhiyan. It had been found that outdoor defecation and a serious lack of private toilets were responsible for many diseases as well as child malnutrition (inability to retain food due to dysentery, etc.). So he launched a campaign for toilets inside the house.

Prime Minister Modi also observed that India's manufacturing had stagnated. When he was the chief minister of Gujarat, he had been unable to travel abroad as he faced visa denial due to the 2002 riots. He had, therefore, begun to invite industrialists and bankers from abroad for a Global Gujarat Summit. He had some success. As the prime minister now, he invited foreign multinationals to locate in India not just to sell to Indian buyers, but also as an export platform. He called it 'Make in India'. He has made digitization a major part of his agenda. The demonetization experiment itself has boosted the use of e-wallets and cashless payment technologies.

Of course, he had to show that his ability to win elections had not been expended. There were state elections soon after he became prime minister. In Delhi itself, which is a union territory (much like Washington, D.C. which has a truncated status rather than a full state), there was an election in which the BJP relied on Modi's appeal. When the results came out, the Aam Aadmi Party (AAP), a recently established grass-roots-based party, had won 67 out of 70 seats with the BJP winning 3 seats and Congress none at all. Worse was to follow. In Bihar, which is a large state sending 40 MPs, a coalition of anti-BJP parties defeated him and this was seen as a vindication of the old-style Congress politics of secularism opposing Modi's suspected anti-Muslim bias.

Soon, the fortunes were to turn. Modi extended the BJP rule to the north-east for the first time by winning Assam, where Congress had won thrice previously. The best was the election in Uttar Pradesh (UP), India's largest state with 140 million voters which sends 80 MPs to the Lok Sabha. The UP election was to take place in seven phases, between early February to 8 March 2017. Thus, the election overlapped with the demonetization experiment. Dire consequences had been predicted with a huge loss of GDP, large-scale unemployment, misery for the poor, etc. The Congress made an alliance with the Samajwadi Party (SP), which was the incumbent. Here was a coalition of anti-BJP forces following the Bihar example. In the event, BJP got three-fourths of the seats with 41.4 per cent of the votes, a swing of 25 percentage points in its favour.

Modi had taken a huge risk by demonetizing. Rather than blame him for what he had done, voters, especially the poorer ones, admired that the step he had taken was inconveniencing the rich as much as them. They had always stood in queues for their rations or healthcare, but they had rarely seen better-off people in queues. This was a redistributive move, a rare one in Indian politics which abounds in rhetoric but lacks action on redistribution. By conventional wisdom, a rightist party like the BJP is not supposed to have redistributive policies. That is the privilege of left, liberal and secular parties in Indian politics. Modi was vindicated when preliminary estimates of GDP growth rate showed that, at most, the growth rate for the fiscal year 2016–17 had gone down by one half of 1 percent—7.1 per cent rather than 7.6 per cent.

Modi, however, is also surprising in many other respects. He has been successful in capturing the Dalit vote across India from its previous champions such as Mayawati and her Bahujan Samaj Party (BSP), which lost 61 out of the 80 seats it had in the previous UP Assembly. The Dalits had decided to vote for the party which gave them hope of advancement rather than just special pleading for them.

In the event, demonetization was a success, albeit after the delay in delivering new currency notes had been dealt with by early March. Many analysts had estimated that a part of the cash hoards would lose value as the holders would shy away from depositing the money in banks, as that would expose them to tax authorities. In fact, 96 per cent of the money came back into the banks. Many black money hoarders recruited poor people as mules. The government had taken an initiative to promote financial inclusion. Twenty-three million new bank accounts had been opened under the Prime Minister's Jan Dhan (people's wealth) accounts scheme. Suddenly, there was an influx of money in these accounts, as much as ₹290 billion at one stage. The government quickly put a limit of ₹50,000 on these accounts which reduced the deposits. What the hoarders also did was to quickly buy gold and jewellery. There were reports of people buying hundreds of airline tickets and foreign currencies from banks to launder their cash. They thwarted the government's desire to devalorize their cash. Had some cash been rendered valueless, that would have reduced the liabilities of the RBI and been made available to the government as a windfall gain. Had a substantial sum come to the government, it could have passed it on to the citizens to fulfil Modi's promise. That was not to be.

The demonetization experiment brought political benefits to Modi as the UP elections showed. Going forward, there will be a clean-up of financial transactions in India and black money transactions will be discouraged. The bank deposits allow tax authorities to chase persons holding black cash and check their tax compliance. It may take more attempts at demonetization before Indians are totally weaned off illegal transactions. But a radical change has been made. The public has been warned. Only a bold prime minister who thinks in an unconventional fashion could have done this.

Modi is an outsider in two senses. He belongs to a low caste, that of an OBC. Even after seventy years, upper-caste members across political parties capture a disproportionate amount of the top positions. Modi was greeted with incredulity and an arrogant dismissal when he was chosen to lead the BJP in the 2014 elections. He lacks the sophistication which the Congress leadership habitually projects. They are educated in the best schools and foreign universities. Modi, on the other hand, had received his degree through a correspondence course. There is a constant doubt expressed by many politicians about the authenticity of his degree, somewhat like the saga about Obama's birth certificate in USA.

When he won the 2014 elections, Modi was also an outsider to Delhi and its political culture. Somewhat like the Beltway in USA, there is a certain code of conduct for a politician in Delhi. There are deals to be made with the opposition. Modi was innocent of this and also reluctant to make deals; in this, he is very unlike Trump. The BJP lacked a majority in the Rajya Sabha, which has members elected by state assemblies proportionate to their strength. As he wins more state elections, the numbers will move in his favour. But he has had a lot of problems getting legislation through both houses.

But unlike Donald Trump, he was not unused to political decision making. He had been chief minister of Gujarat for twelve years and had won thrice. His executive experience has been crucial to his performance as prime minister. State chief ministers can afford to be presidential. Typically, with a majority in the assembly, they normally dominate their cabinet. Modi was able to repeat that behaviour at the Centre. This was because everyone in his party conceded that they had won a majority thanks to the prodigious effort he had made during the election campaign.

Victory in UP more or less guarantees that Modi will win in 2019 too. If there are flies in the ointment, they are due to local actions by vigilante groups who want to enforce an anti-Muslim agenda. The cause they claim to defend is the cow, holy to Hindus. They attack anyone transporting cattle. Cattle trade and especially the meat industry—slaughterhouses and butcher shops—are predominantly Muslim activities. Thus, when cattle is being transported by Muslims, the vigilante groups attack, often killing the person transporting. Law and order is a State Subject, not a federal one. Local police are often themselves not impartial. Modi has criticized these cow protection vigilante groups, but that has not stemmed the problem. No matter how far away from Delhi it happens, Modi gets the blame. Modi's detractors are still in denial. They find it hard to believe (rather like the detractors of Donald Trump) that their true and tried model does not work any more.

For the first time since Jawaharlal Nehru, the first prime minister of India, India's position in global affairs is high. Modi has travelled the world ceaselessly to establish the image of India as a dynamic economy as well as a success being the world's largest democracy. He has championed an opening to Asia much more vigorously than previous governments have done. The leaders of Japan and China have visited India, and Modi has reciprocated. He secured friendship with Obama and is expected to get along with Donald Trump.

Modi surprised his detractors and even his supporters when he invited the prime minister of Pakistan, Nawaz Sharif, at the swearing-in ceremony of his government. As he was thought to be anti-Muslim, people had expected him to be virulently anti-Pakistan. His gesture showed that Modi, like Trump, is his own man. He does not fit people's preconceptions.

Modi's main battleground has been at home, in Parliament. Having a majority in the lower house is not enough except for money bills which, as per the British tradition, are the monopoly of the lower house. Not having a majority in the upper house has been a factor slowing down the government. It is not only that passage of bills takes longer. The Indian Parliament is not a well-behaved, decorous assembly. Members shout, leave their seats and rush to the well of the chamber. The speaker in the lower house and the vice president presiding over the upper house have little control over the members. More often, no business gets transacted because of some protest about some recent news. In these circumstances, the Modi team has had to learn to tread carefully and build consensus. The new government failed to repeal and replace the Land Acquisition Act of the previous government which makes it very difficult to acquire land for industrial or infrastructure projects. That episode early in its term taught it to proceed with caution in getting its legislation passed.

But just in March 2017, the government was able to pass the Goods and Services Tax (GST) Act. This legislation has been under discussion under Congress as well as the BJP for fifteen years. Its passage revolutionizes the Indian economy by establishing a single market with a uniform indirect tax structure. Until now, numerous local taxes and restrictions had slowed down the movement of goods across the states, which also makes it expensive in the process. Now the unification of the tax structure will add considerably to the ease of doing business and bring costs down.

Modi has also reinforced his leadership quality by being a good communicator round the year, and not just during election times. He has an active Twitter account. Citizens are encouraged to go directly to his website. He has a monthly radio talk show *Mann ki Baat* (What Is on My Mind). He travels around the country and takes a lead role in every election campaign. People see him and hear him all the time. That is a lot different from previous prime ministers.

Trump's First Hundred Days and After

If Modi has been able to achieve much in his first thousand days (demonetization happened on the 938th day after his election on 16 May 2014), Donald Trump has not been able to set the pace he wanted to when he came to power. The contrast between Modi and Trump is interesting. In popular imagination, and no doubt in Trump's own mind, the US presidency is one of the most powerful positions. We are often given the impression of the American president's power in terms of his ability to push the nuclear button. On his campaign trail, Trump made promises of what he would accomplish in office as soon as he got elected. He was to build a wall to keep Mexican immigrants out, repeal and replace Obamacare, inaugurate an infrastructure building programme and offer a massive tax cut. He was to reconsider various trade treaties America had signed, and declared China to be a currency manipulator.

What Trump had not realized was that the American Constitution was written by people who distrusted executive power. Having battled against what they saw as the mistaken policies of George the Third, they did not want a monarchical president. There is a separation of powers between the executive, the legislature and the judiciary, not just on paper but in real practice. In the British Constitution, the prime minister with a majority in Parliament works through the legislature and is, in effect, much more powerful. The president is hobbled at each turn, except in foreign policy where he has considerable room for unilateral action.

Trump discovered the power of the judiciary at once when he passed an executive order restricting travellers from seven Muslim-majority countries on the grounds that terrorists had to be kept out. His order was stopped by the courts. His promise to build a wall requires Congress to sanction the money by passing an Appropriation Bill. In American budgetary procedure, the fiscal year runs from October to September. Obama's last budget message related to the budget for October 2016 to September 2017. The money for the first six months was spoken for by the Appropriation

Bills already passed by the Congress. There had to be a bill passed to allow spending beyond the first six months or the government would shut down (as has happened a few times recently). On the 101st day, Congress was able to pass the necessary legislation for the spending to continue. As it required the cooperation of the Democrats, no money was sanctioned for the wall.

An incoming president has to make around 5,000 appointments to fill the vacancies created by the changeover from the previous administration. Trump has been slow in filling these slots. He has filled a few top slots but Congressional hearings have been slow in approving them. He does, however, have his Secretaries of State, Treasury, Commerce, Labour and Energy. Many of the economic appointments have drawn on Goldman Sachs alumni, who have put some realism in Trump's policies. Thus, he has not called China a currency manipulator and had a fruitful meeting with President Xi Jinping at his Florida White House. He has maintained good relations with Prime Minister Abe of Japan. He has resiled from unilaterally scrapping NAFTA, but insists on renegotiating it with Canada and Mexico.

Trump has fully used the room that the separation of powers allows the president in foreign policy. He has intervened in Syria when he found evidence that the Assad regime had used chemical weapons. When the same situation confronted the West four years ago, Obama followed the British example—he sought the agreement of the legislature knowing full well it would not be forthcoming. He did not need that agreement. Trump was able to move in on humanitarian grounds saying children had been killed by Assad. He also used the largest non-nuclear bomb in America's arsenal in Afghanistan against Daesh forces. This was also his way of warning

North Korea that USA could destroy its underground bunkers any time it chose to.

Trump has worried foreign policy professionals because, as in everything else, he plays by his own rules. This makes him unpredictable, which is a problem for American foreign policy experts, but even a greater problem for the rest of the world. He complained about the fiscal burden America was bearing providing NATO cover for European countries. He complained they were not doing their bit and spending less than the pledged 2 per cent of GDP on defence. This shocked the Allies because they feared Trump may dismantle the alliance. But his actions in Syria and Afghanistan show that he is not an isolationist. He is a unilateralist. He does things without consulting anyone outside his own very small circle of advisers, prominent among whom are his daughter Ivanka and her husband Jared Kushner.

Trump has also been quicker than Obama in dealing with North Korea. He has built up a rapport with Xi Jinping despite his hostile anti-China comments during the campaign. China is the only power to whom Kim Jong-Un listens. It is an initiative Trump has taken to tackle the difficult problem of North Korean nuclear capability. He cannot either hope for a regime change nor can he let things continue as they are. Obama's policy of strategic patience failed to change Kim's behaviour. Any attempt to unseat him would lead to retaliation against Japan and South Korea. So there has to be a negotiated detente. Trump surprised everyone by saying, 'It would be an honour' to meet Kim Jong-Un. An American president declaring it an honour to see a renegade Asian leader raised eyebrows. But Trump is a deal maker and he knows he has to get a deal with Kim to remove the nuclear threat.

In the same way, despite his campaign rhetoric against Muslims and his executive order (overturned by lower courts) to restrict entry into USA for travellers from Muslim nations, he has been to Riyadh for a meeting with Saudi Arabia and other Middle Eastern Muslim countries. He was able to conclude trade agreements worth hundreds of billions selling arms to Saudi Arabia. He was carefully eloquent when addressing a conference of Muslim nations of the Gulf by speaking of Islam with respect, but sharply contrasting the Islamist terrorist as the common enemy. His Middle East trip was his maiden travel abroad as president. He belied the fears people had about his capacity of casually giving offence. Trump abroad was truly diplomatic unlike Trump at home.

Trump is a classic populist. He believes he represents the real people. Their urges and anxieties are taken up by him uncritically as valid. He genuinely thinks in headlines and instant action; hence, his stand on the wall with Mexico or denouncing China as a currency manipulator. But he is finding out that in the real world there are inevitable delays before you can get things done, and life is not black and white. He will need the cooperation of Congress as well as the international community to accomplish what he desires. He will not only visit Israel, but even the Palestinian Authority will meet him. As he is an unknown and unpredictable quantity, leaders of other countries know that knowing him personally is essential.

Trump has two solid achievements to his credit. He was able to nominate Judge Neil Gorsuch to fill the vacancy in the Supreme Court. The Republicans overcame the threat of a filibuster by the Democrats by changing the rule that instead of requiring a 60/40 vote, a simple majority, which they had, would be enough. This is a major and permanent change in the procedure, and no doubt the

Democrats will use it to their advantage when they are back in power.

The other success is with the reform of Obamacare. The Affordable Care Act passed by Obama was the first piece of legislation extending healthcare insurance to a large number of people. Of all the G7 countries, USA is alone in not having a comprehensive health insurance scheme. But it remains contested. The House of Representatives voted with a majority of 213 to 211 to replace the Affordable Care Act by a new legislation on 4 May 2017. It will have to pass the Senate, but Trump was able to claim that he had delivered on his campaign promise almost within the first hundred days.

Trump has been watched closely. This is partly because he has antagonized many in the media by accusing them of peddling 'fake news'. His style of tweeting at various times of the day and night and even contradicting himself has also bewildered his friends and amused his critics. This has meant that anything and everything he does gets a negative or at best an unenthusiastic presentation. This has not stopped him from being what he is but the reported news does need a lot of filtering. There have also been almost non-stop demonstrations and marches against him. The Trump presidency has been the least popular if polls are to be believed.

Trump has barely begun his presidency. He has 1,460 days in all; so the first hundred or two hundred days do not matter too much. Much will depend on whether he achieves his goal of making infrastructure investments. That will raise the economic growth rate of USA significantly. His tax cut remains controversial because it depends on the gamble that the extra growth it will generate will avert any budget deficit. Trump has been the most fiscally active politician in the way he has argued so far. After almost a decade of fiscal austerity and loose monetary policy, America and the world are ready for a change. If Trump succeeds, he may get re-elected. That sounds outrageously optimistic for Trump, but it is not beyond the bounds of possibility.

Populism and Liberal Democracy

Trump's election has brought the notion of populism in the general debate. America had a populist movement in the nineteenth century which was radical. But contemporary discussion of populism casts it as divisive, anti-pluralism and proto-fascist.* Populists describe a part of the population as 'real' or 'authentic', by implication dismissing the rest, often the elite but sometimes people of a different race or religion as not real. This is regardless of numbers. The populist emphasizes that he represents the good, the hard working and the deserving while the rest are effete, elitist and corrupt.

Populists can be left or right oriented. Mussolini began as a socialist before founding a fascist movement. Hitler pretended to be left by calling his party National Socialist German Workers Party. Trump is nowhere near either of them, whatever his caricaturists may say. What is more, as we have already seen, his power to enact laws or implement policies is severely limited by separation of powers. The populist may command a majority (Trump does not), but even so that is not enough unless he commands a huge and obedient majority in the Congress. The protection against the bad outcomes of populism is the diversity of opinion within the several institutions of the government. This is even more the case with an independent judiciary.

---

*Jan-Wener Mueller. 2016. *What Is Populism?* Philadelphia: University of Pennsylvania Press.

It is fashionable among the Indian liberal media to invoke the name of Hitler when speaking of Modi, but it is misleading for many reasons. First of all, Modi is not a populist. As a member of the BJP and a lifelong volunteer of the RSS, he has a Hindu outlook on politics. This may make him a majoritarian, but not a populist. Yet, Modi has been careful in insisting on an inclusive message in his many speeches. It may be argued that this inclusiveness wears thin when it comes to the issue of Muslims. Certainly, within the BJP there are people who would wish to isolate, exile or eliminate Muslims. But that has not been any part of Modi's policy or rhetoric.

There is, however, a different argument why neither populism nor majoritarianism will work in India. This is because of India's much-valued diversity. Germany and Italy had relatively homogeneous people with the majority as Christians and Jews were in the minority. They spoke the same language. In India, though Hindus are an overwhelming majority (80 per cent), there are differences among them. India has twenty-eight languages officially and hundred and more unofficial languages, with around seven thousand dialects. A North Indian person speaking Hindi and Punjabi will not understand a word of South Indian languages such as Tamil, Telugu, Malayalam or Kannada, or even East Indian languages such as Assamese. The idea that religion binds people together was exploded when East Pakistan seceded from Pakistan and became Bangladesh in 1971. Within twenty-five years of its foundation as a Muslim nation state, Pakistan broke up because the Bengali-speaking East Pakistani Muslim could not get along with the Urdu- or Punjabi-speaking Muslim of West Pakistan. Hindus are not a homogeneous community, unlike the Han people in China. Diversity of language, region and caste defines several sections among them. Jinnah misunderstood India when he thought that a permanent Hindu majority will confront a Muslim minority. He also misinterpreted what made Muslims a community. As Bangladesh proves, Muslims are no more a community bound by religion than Hindus are. In the Middle East, over the last few years, more Muslims have been killed by their fellow Muslims on the grounds of religion than on any other ideology. Before the Muslims came to India, there was no political unity among the kingdoms. Indeed, the typical story of those centuries is division among the Hindus.

Modi has been aware of this. Previously, the BJP faced a barrier and could only get 182 seats at best in successive elections. Modi saw that an exclusively Hindu agenda was not enough. This is why he has adopted an inclusive slogan of *Sabka Saath, Sabka Vikas*. As I mentioned above, he has actively sought the Dalit vote, whereas the orthodox Hindu would shrink from such a possibility. In UP, there was never any question of the BJP winning Dalit votes till Modi came to the scene. As a lower-caste Hindu, he can empathize with the downtrodden Dalits.

Populism is not, therefore, a simple category. We may find the populist odious as a political phenomenon. Trump used a populist rhetoric to defeat one of the most formidable candidates. But it is clear from even the first hundred days that he will not rule as a populist. Come 2020, he may fight elections again using the same rhetoric, but his actions would be different.

Modi is thus not easily described as a populist or worse as a fascist. He has so far shown himself as a democrat. His message of inclusion has helped the BJP win more state elections than it has lost. To win elections across different regions of India, the politician has to create coalitions of voters, different by caste, religion and economic status. He has to be genuinely inclusive.

Indian elections are, of course, a totally different experience from anything in Western democracies. The electorate is large; it was 850 million in 2014 and will no doubt hit a billion soon. Given the size of the country, an election has to be spread over several weeks, though electronic voting machines (EVMs) do speed up the counting once all the ballots have been conducted. The turnout is usually in the 60–70 per cent range. Even more remarkable is the fact that the poor vote more assiduously than the better-off voters, whereas in Western countries it is often the opposite. You also have to deal with scores of parties, though many are local and small. The Lok Sabha had 49 parties in the 2009–14 period. The electorate is diverse by language, caste, economic circumstance, levels of literacy, etc. Regional identities are strong. In Tamil Nadu, only local parties have been in ruling positions for the last fifty years.

There are 'vote banks' formed by specific jatis (sub-castes) many of which can swing elections. Over the last twenty-five years, the recruitment of vote banks by way of the local strength of the jatis has determined the fortunes of some parties. Thus, in UP, the Yadavs are a large OBC community. They form the backbone of the SP, which has been in power several times. The Yadavs are also spread over other states. Thus, it would be necessary to invite a UP Yadav leader if you were fighting elections in Delhi where there is a Yadav population.

While fighting elections in any state, one would need to know the detailed census data as to which jatis have strength and which ones are friendly or antagonistic to the other. Yet, the electorate is not static. With economic development young voters are going away from their jati identity and seeking opportunities which will take them out of the confines of the old structures. Modi has seen this, and he has tried to appeal to voters across the jati and religious divide.

A successful leader weaves a complex quilt of diverse communities, age groups and regional identities to gain power. It is this diversity which has nourished Indian democracy.

FOUR

ECONOMICS AND POLITICS OF NATIONALISM

The election of Donald Trump has led to many reactions, mostly negative, from the LO. One major strand of this negative reaction concerns the revival/return of nationalism, especially economic nationalism. Sometimes, it is called populism. The economic meaning attached to those terms is that the multilateral liberal trade arrangement under WTO rules will be interfered with or abandoned. There is the prospect that Trump may adopt a protectionist stance and disown or destroy international trade agreements. In 1992, Ross Perot fought the US presidential election on the sole topic of opposing the NAFTA. Doubts about the benefits of trade treaties were also the theme of Bernie Sanders's campaign. There is here a convergence between the right and left. So what is economic nationalism, and why is it so controversial?

The Prizes and Pitfalls of Economic Nationalism

The modern world can be said to have been inaugurated in the final decade of the fifteenth century when the Iberian kingdoms 'discovered' America and India. The conquest of Mexico and South America by the Spaniards led to a huge outflow of gold and silver from South America to Spain. This accumulation of gold was much envied by other European powers. They sponsored pirates to loot the Spanish ships on high seas, but even so Spain amassed much 'treasure'. As inflation picked up in Spain, it imported a lot of goods from outside and began to lose its gold in payment for imports. The debate about foreign trade then converged on the idea that nations should export as much as possible and earn gold to accumulate treasure, but import very little. This was called mercantilism. Adam Smith (1723–90) in his classic work *An Inquiry into the Nature and Causes of the Wealth of Nations* (1776) argued that this was not a policy to enhance well-being. If everyone exported and no one imported, there soon would be no trade. What was more, countries needed to import stuff they couldn't easily produce at home. They should export what they did best and import goods which were costly for them to make. That way, both their total income and the satisfaction of their citizen–consumers would be higher.

It was David Ricardo (1772–1823) who sharpened this idea fifty years after Smith in the early nineteenth century. Unlike Adam Smith, who was an academic and an unworldly philosopher, Ricardo was a man of the world. He did not finish school. At the age of fourteen, he had to join his father working on the London Stock Exchange. In his middle years, he became interested in economic questions starting with inflation. England had gone off the gold standard during the war with Napoleon and had begun to use paper currency. The pound depreciated. Ricardo proposed that the depreciation of the pound relative to the Dutch florin was a good measure of excess currency issued by the government. It set off a long debate and Parliament appointed a committee to examine the problem which vindicated Ricardo. He continued to think about economic issues in the course of a busy life, which included being an MP as well as a stockbroker, landlord and writer.

Two hundred years ago in 1817, Ricardo published his classic work *Principles of Political Economy and Taxation*. The book became the authoritative work for the rest of the century. His enduring contribution has been the proposition that in international trade, countries should specialize in what they can do *comparatively* better than other things. In his famous example of England and Portugal trading with each other and wine and cloth being the two goods, even if Portugal can make both wine and cloth cheaper than England, it should concentrate on that which it can make cheaper of the two and import the other. In his example, it takes eighty men in Portugal to make wine and ninety men to make cloth (the quantity of each is taken as standard). England can make cloth with hundred men and wine with 120 men. While Portugal can make both cheaper than England, it should specialize in wine where it has a *comparative* advantage.

As Ricardo put it, 'Under a system of free competition, each country naturally devoted its capital and labour to such employments as are beneficial to both. The pursuit of individual advantage is admirably connected with the universal good of the whole.'*

---

*David Ricardo. 2006. *Principles of Political Economy and Taxation*. USA: Synergy International of the Americas.

Free trade between the two countries, each specializing in the thing in which it had comparative advantage, would make both better off. This idea can then be extended to all countries of the whole world trading with each other. The notion of comparative advantage is so counterintuitive that most non-economists find it incomprehensible.

Ricardo had another great idea which led to a veritable economic revolution within thirty years of his writing his great book. He argued that the rent on land which was the source of income of the landlords, the most powerful class of his days, was a result not of their ability or investment. Over time, the best lands were captured first. As population rose, inferior lands came into cultivation. The cost of growing corn (wheat as we would say now) was higher on the inferior land, but the output was needed to meet the higher demand. The landlords gained because their lands were superior, and their cost of production was lower. The difference between the higher price/cost of corn on the inferior lands and the low cost of superior lands was a pure surplus. Land was in fixed supply and became scarcer relative to population. Thus, the landlords' incomes rose over time.

The combination of these two ideas—import that which is cheaper abroad and that landlords' income is an unearned surplus—combined to set off a radical political movement in England in the mid-nineteenth century. There was a restriction on import of corn, unless the price was above a certain limit. High price of corn meant higher wages of industrial workers, which ate into profits of industrialists. Thus began the Anti-Corn Law movement which argued for free trade in corn. Workers saw the advantage of cheaper bread. They joined with the industrialists to argue for removal of the Corn Law. Landlords were politically powerful but the popular agitation won, and Britain became wedded to free trade in grain. Wheat began to come in from Central Europe and America. British capitalism became a champion of free trade. The working class also became a fervent supporter of free trade, which meant a cheap loaf. Tariffs were zero in UK after the 1850s. The British practised free trade *unilaterally*.

Ricardo's argument became the standard doctrine as much due to England's early start in the Industrial Revolution as its lead in establishing a maritime empire. The other countries of Europe, especially Germany, complained that the theory was not universally true. It was just English national interest parading as universal truth. Countries just beginning to industrialize could not compete with England. They needed to protect their markets with tariffs. America, as a new entrant to manufacturing in the nineteenth century, relied on tariffs to build its industry. Germany and America built up their industries behind a wall of tariff. When, at the turn of the nineteenth century, Great Britain faced competition from Germany and USA, there began a debate about the need for tariffs to protect British manufactures. In the event though, the free traders won out. Thanks to the solid support from workers for free trade, Britain stayed with its Ricardian principles. It wobbled again during the Great Depression of the 1930s and tried Imperial Preference, importing goods from the empire and putting tariffs on foreign goods. It gave this up after the Second World War.

USA used tariffs through the nineteenth century to build up its manufacturing base. It only became a champion of free trade after it became the most industrialized country, following the Second World War. In this, it behaved much like England. One could even set up a historical cycle for nations regarding free trade. A nation beginning to industrialize (USA and Germany in the second half of the nineteenth century and most developing countries after 1945) wants to use tariffs against imports of manufactures from countries with a longer experience of manufacturing (Great Britain). Once it gets to maturity as an industrial nation, especially if it is in the lead (Great Britain in the first half of the nineteenth century, USA after 1945), it propagates free trade. When it matures and faces newly industrializing countries as competitors, it wants to use tariffs or non-tariff barriers. Trump has now taken this view. While asserting American superiority, he has expressed fear and resentment of China's competition. He wants to revise treaties or discourage American manufacturers from locating abroad. China, on the other hand, as President Xi said at Davos on his first visit in January 2017, wishes to champion free trade. This reversal is not surprising when you see that in terms of the value of merchandise exports, China has risen from the rank of eleven in 1997 to one in 2015. America was at the top in 1997 and slipped to two by 2015.*

Economists have convinced themselves about the unrivalled benefits of free trade, but perhaps not the politicians. Economists hope all countries of the world would trade with each other, free of all restrictions on imports or exports, labour or capital. While free trade remains a utopia for economists, politicians are somewhat wary of unrestricted free trade. Hence, there are proposals for *freer trade*, which urges the need to avoid (or keep as low as possible) tariffs, quotas or any non-tariff barriers to trade. The idea is also

---

*'Global Shifts Give Xi Chance to Steal Limelight in Davos', https://article.wn.com/view/2017/01/16/Global_shifts_give_Xi_chance_to_steal_limelight_in_Davos/, accessed 11 June 2017.

to treat all nations with which you are trading face equal treatment, be it in terms of tariffs or other, hopefully minimal, restrictions.

Solutions which combine limited free trade with protection for local industry have always appealed to politicians, though economists frown on them as 'second best'. Customs unions are formed to allow free trade within the Union, but with tariffs for the countries outside the customs union. The EU is a customs union. It is something of a puzzle that the defenders of globalization and liberal trade consider the EU a good development and protectionism a bad thing. But a customs union is a protectionist device against outsiders while allowing free trade within. Indeed, the idea of a customs union was pursued in continental Europe as a defence against British industrial superiority. Zollverein, as it was called, was inspired by the work of Friedrich List (1789–1846), a German economist who migrated to America and wrote the book *The National System of Political Economy*, which argued a nationalist case against the Ricardian free trade doctrine. The great achievement of the EU, as it has gone over the last fifty years through various stages such as EEC, EC and then EU, has been to make possible the re-emergence of Germany as a manufacturing power. The envelope of a customs union has helped.

Other arrangements of closer trade between countries with low tariffs are made by signing Free Trade Agreements (FTAs) bilaterally, or Regional Trade Agreements (RTAs) multilaterally, such as NAFTA. These are devices to reap the benefits of trade without losing control over global competition. The WTO would prefer no such partial schemes, but a level playing field with trade of all with all.

Who Gains and Who Loses?

But while freer trade benefits all parties, the division of the gains from trade can be uneven. In the Anti-Corn Law agitation, the landlords lost their rental income while workers got cheap bread (higher real wages) and industrialists got better profits as wages did not have to keep up with food price inflation. In our days, from the 1990s onwards, China gained in the manufacturing output and employment areas (somewhat thanks to American and other foreign capital migrating to China for profits), while USA suffered a shrinkage in the same areas. Americans, all of them, benefited from cheaper manufactures. Companies which had invested in manufacturing in China made better profits. The loss of jobs and income was confined to a minority in the Midwest. In an ideal world, the gainers (American consumers and capital exporters) would compensate the losers (American workers who lost their jobs). Indeed the economist would say that one could judge a trade policy to be beneficial only if after the change the gainers could compensate the losers and still have something for themselves. But no one actually compensates. The consumers gain, but they do not feel an increase in the money in their pockets, just lower shopping bills. The landlords who lost from the abolition of Corn Laws never got compensated by the industrialists or workers. Those who exported capital to China felt they have done the right thing as entrepreneurs. The gainers never thought they owe the losers.

The anti-trade rhetoric, therefore, concentrates not on gainers and losers within a country, but on the country which has gained in trade vis-à-vis their home country which they reckon has lost out. It sees trade as a zero sum game; your gain is my loss. It says that the party which gained in output and employment (China) should compensate the losers (American workers). This is much more likely to win political support because the party responsible for the loss is a foreigner and obviously the gainer in terms of jobs.

Developing countries were allowed to use tariffs and protection to nurse their infant industries. It was only after the oil shock of the 1970s that enough of them were able to industrialize to seek entry into Western markets. They were able to compete, and within thirty years had captured a large share of the global manufacturing trade. Except for Great Britain, which industrialized without tariffs, thanks to its first-mover advantage, every other nation which currently qualifies as industrialized has used tariffs to get where it is. The paradox of the LO is that it wants to preserve the present, almost tariff free, world, but has forgotten that we arrived here climbing with the help of tariffs.

Even as economists warn about a lurch into protectionism, we must bear in mind that agriculture is highly protected everywhere, most of all in USA. The EU has a common agricultural policy, which until the turn of the century was highly restrictive, and resulted in surplus output—wine lakes and beef mountains. There were also allegations that the surplus output was dumped on to Third World economies, ruining their agriculture. The policy has been reformed and made more environmentally friendly, but remains protectionist.

Though anti-trade rhetoric may be politically popular, does it make economic sense? Globalization, which came into its latest upswing in the 1990s, regards all interferences with free trade as a serious departure from economic rationality. This can be a view held by the economies which are industrially mature and able to withstand competition. It is also the case in the last thirty years that supply chains in many manufactured products have crossed national boundaries. Thus, a car-maker in USA may get its engines from Mexico or Canada or even Germany. The older idea of an industry fully producing within the boundaries—of a self-sufficient industrial nation—has been overtaken by the superior logic of specialization across national boundaries. This fragmentation of the production process has become possible due to new technology. The Silicon Valley revolution has allowed the design of a product to be made in one place and the assembly to be made in another location far away, after coordinating the supply chain spanning several other countries.

There has been a greater concern with inequality of income and wealth lately. Many people have connected the present disenchantment with globalization with its effect on equality. But the nostrum suggested, such as a global income tax, is neither practical nor does it locate the correct problem. It is not the income inequality across the entire population but division between many gainers and some losers which is at the core of the distribution problem. The need is to devise ways which will transfer some of the gain to the losers. Thus, if the benefit is in the form of cheaper manufactures, a sales tax would garner revenue which could be spent on re-skilling the losers from globalization in the form of a sort of GI bill. It would be better than the border adjustment tax, a tax on imports in fact. The latter will hurt importers in the country, including retailers and industries which use the imports as inputs. Attracting the old industries back to USA, as Trump proposes, will neither help the losers nor the economy. In a dynamic context, the good strategist would rather try to launch new industries with high demand than reintroduce an obsolete industry in which there is already oversupply, such as steel. Protectionism has to be smart to deliver, not sentimental.

Even at the height of globalization and the LO, there has never been a borderless world. We do not have a global economy. We have an interstate community in which gains and losses are measured in national terms. There is perhaps an elite which is globally mobile and can work and live in any country or even many countries. For them, it is 'One World'. The elite, individually or through their corporate entity choose to pay their income or corporation taxes where they are the lowest. Only the very well-offs or the larger corporations can do this. But, for the overwhelming majority of the world, life, work and happiness as well as taxation are local. The tension is even greater because the income differences between countries are huge. The LO is an order of the relatively affluent, developed countries. Even so, within each of these countries, there is income inequality and, consequently, uneven benefits derived from trade. The benevolent attitude towards freer trade, which the better-offs have, is not shared by those at the bottom. This may be irrational on the part of the poor as they enjoy cheaper goods or perhaps even their jobs, thanks to foreign trade. But what we have seen lately is a louder articulation of that contrary view.

The issue then is of the distribution of gains from trade *within* a country and *among* trading countries. There is no doubt that in the latest phases of globalization, say, from 1990 to 2007, the gains were large enough to 'trickle down' to the bottom and keep people happy with the changes. Poverty was drastically reduced in China and India and other Asian countries, which could export to Western markets, while the poor in the rich countries were enjoying full employment, cheap credit and cheaper manufactures. If one takes countries as individuals, there is no doubt that inter-country inequality has been reduced while intra-country inequality in developed countries has increased. Governments had connived in this increasing inequality as much by doing nothing to counter it. They had further adopted policies which protected the rich and abandoned the poor. Thus, banks which had made disastrous investments were rescued at taxpayers' expense, but government budgets were subjected to a strict discipline of cutting debts and deficits, which meant austerity and hardships for the less well-off. Governments conspired in these inegalitarian policies in the name of free market policies. Monetary policy was made extremely loose. The effect was to lower interest rates drastically till they were nudging zero. Banks and corporations received lot of cash which was reinvested in emerging markets in risky, high-yielding assets. For those who could afford, hedge funds and other asset management companies promised and delivered high returns. Incomes of those in the top decile and even more the top percentile increased.

Piketty in his bestseller *Capital in the Twenty-First Century* presents persuasive evidence for the growing inequality. His evidence also tells us that over the century-long data, we can see cycles in inequality of income. There was a peak in inequality during the first quarter of the twentieth century and then a downward movement through the Great Depression and post-war period. It was only after the oil shock of 1973 and the outward migration of manufacturing from advanced capitalist countries that we witness rising inequality again.

Piketty advocates progressive taxation on a global scale. It is doubtful that such a proposal is politically feasible. But even if it were, it fails to address the malaise that has become manifest in recent political shocks. The dissatisfaction with inequality is not generic.

It is specific to the groups who perceive themselves as losers due to trade. Their grievances need a much more specific and focused attack than global progressive taxation.

The economics of Donald Trump is a response to the neglected issue of distribution of gains from trade. Economists firmly believe that protectionism is a false God. To encourage production at home of what you could import cheaper may generate jobs, but it will be at the cost of higher costs and inefficiency. There is also the fear that if Trump uses tariffs or the 'bully pulpit' to discourage imports, and locates industries at home to replace imports, other countries may retaliate. Then USA would suffer a reduction in its exports. Soon, there will be a downward spiral. This was what happened during the Great Depression with the infamous Smoot–Hawley tariffs. The Smoot–Hawley tariffs were imposed in 1930 whereby America raised tariffs on 20,000 imported items. The tariff levels were the second highest in US history, exceeded only by the tariffs of 1828. There was retaliation by other countries. American exports went down more than its imports, and this led to a deepening of the Depression. After the war, USA was committed to establishing a liberal trading regime with a progressive joint reduction in tariffs by the developed countries under the General Agreement on Tariffs and Trade (GATT).

If Donald Trump tries to use protectionism or high tariffs, he will encounter opposition in the US Congress itself. There are also obligations under WTO rules to avoid such policies. The issue though is: Will he make America better off if he does succeed in getting these policies past the Congress? If he does re-employ all those former coal miners or industrial workers whose industry has shut down, will America gain or lose on balance? No doubt, it will have the effect of making goods more expensive if made at home rather than imported. The extra employment of some may lead to unemployment in the importing industries. Add to this, possible retaliatory effects.

The answer is neither obvious nor clear cut. If in four years' time having implemented protectionist policies with all their consequences on the American and the global economy Trump gets re-elected, it has to be labelled a political success. It is a crude way of solving the problem of the distribution of gains from trade, but if the policy wins political approval (granting all the deficiencies of the Electoral College arrangement), who is to say he did wrong?

There is this inescapable tension between economic calculus, which leaves political considerations out, and the world of politics in which economic benefits do count but often in ways economists do not approve of. USA may be better off, or some Americans may be, the economist would say, but what about the world? Is this not a policy reducing global welfare? The politician would say the world does not vote for me; my fellow countrymen and women do. As Donald Trump put it once again in his inaugural address, 'America First'.

There have been cycles of free trade followed by protection. Thus, if the first seventy-five years of the nineteenth century were protectionist, there was a period of globalization in the final quarter and up to the start of the First World War. With the gold standard, there was virtually a single currency or predictable fixed exchange rates. It was during this period that London emerged as the global financial centre where countries from around the world could raise capital for their projects. The climate of liberalism and free trade was such as can bear comparison with what happened during a similar period, 1990–2016.

Indeed, this period at the cusp of the end of the nineteenth and the beginning of the twentieth century—*Belle Époque*, as it was called—raised hopes of eternal peace. Norman Angell wrote in his bestselling book *The Great Illusion* that economic interdependence among European countries was such that war would be unprofitable and futile. European nations should get out of the illusion that war and territorial conquest would help the victor. This was a sort of faith in the LO, a peaceful world of mutual economic benefits of trade. Then, within five years of his writing the book, European nations did indulge in their illusion, and plunged into a very damaging conflict. One could say the war vindicated Angell's warning or that he was too naive to believe that mere economic loss would discourage nations from fighting each other.

Either way, the liberal trade regime of the 1875–1914 era disappeared during the interwar period. The interwar period (1919–45) saw a break-up of globalization, the onset of tariff wars and the collapse of the gold standard. The idea that protection by one country is inevitably the beginning of a mutual war of protection and tariffs comes from this period. But we can point to earlier periods that this did not happen even when many countries did use tariffs. Whether Trump's intended policy leads to a downward spiral of tariff wars, as in the 1919–39 period, or a mutual accommodation, as in the nineteenth century, is a matter of conjecture.

A second aspect of nationalism concerns immigrants—whether they are refugees, asylum seekers or just economic migrants. Most people favour free movement of goods, services and capital. It is when it comes to labour that objections mount against free movement. Brexit was all about the resentment many Britishers felt about the migration of EU citizens into UK without any control. This is the fear UKIP played on. Historically, USA has been the most open economy, welcoming immigrants from around the world. But there is a prejudice against Mexicans who have been able to enter USA illegally. Trump has zeroed in on this issue. Obama's desire to regularize the situation of illegal immigrants was the true liberal position.

In the view of some political leaders, Chancellor Angela Merkel, for instance, there is a humanitarian case for rich countries to welcome and accommodate refugees from war-torn countries. Not everyone shares this view, even within the EU. But there are also economic migrants who leave their poor home countries and try to enter rich countries, where they could be better off. These economic migrants are illegal, but desperate enough to sail across the seas from Africa to Europe. Obviously, a huge influx of migrants from poor countries into rich ones would lower wages and hurt the bottom rung of native workers in the host country. The argument is complicated if migrants take risks with their lives, and especially if children with them face extreme hardships.

There is no doubt that within the LO, nationalism is viewed with fear and dislike. This is not in USA alone. The EU has been created to slay the old demon of nationalism, which in view of its creators was the cause of two destructive wars. The EU aims to build a post-nationalist Union. This is why it is border free and guarantees free movement of all citizens of member countries across all countries of the union. The single currency adds to this feeling of solidarity.

This dream was jolted when UK voted in a referendum on 23 June 2016 to exit the EU. The bone of contention was the free movement of EU workers across the Union. As far as the British were concerned, these immigrants were foreigners and not any more welcome than any other migrants. As these were fellow Europeans and, therefore, mostly white, the objection was due to xenophobia, rather than racism. UK had seen race riots and racial discrimination during the 1950s, 1960s and 1970s. It had taken a long time of patient social work backed by law and policing to reduce racism. Even so, it was never fully eliminated. But the anger about the Romanians and Bulgarians was something else again. It was this anger which was one of the driving forces behind Brexit.

Brexit is an assertion of British, even more English, nationalism which surprised many Europhiles in UK itself. English nationalism is a peculiar phenomenon. There is very little overt expression of nationalism in England. There is a warm feeling for the royalty among the conservatives. The left has traditionally been not enthusiastic about the royalty but not nationalist either. If anything, it is mildly internationalist and embarrassed by nationalism. English nationalism springs from the right wing, a preoccupation of empire loyalists who are nostalgic and angry about the loss of the empire. The influx of the citizens of the Commonwealth during the post-war period, from the Caribbean and African colonies and later from South Asia and East Africa, incited racist sentiments. The infamous speech by Enoch Powell, MP, in 1968, warning about rivers of blood which may flow due to the influx of black immigrants marked a low point in racism. But, by the turn of the century, there had been a remarkable degree of multiracial integration in the UK. Examples of virulent racism had subsided, though not been totally eliminated. When young Muslim men went on to join ISIS, the headlines were all about British youth led astray or our boys joining the jihadists rather than denigrating them as 'Pakis', which would have been the case thirty years previously. After the referendum, there was a revival of racist attacks which shocked the country.

Not all nationalism is right wing. Scottish nationalism has always had a left radical ideology. Scottish nationalism has had a revival in the last twenty-five years and the Scottish Nationalist Party (SNP) aspires to win the vote for an independent Scotland, thus ending the Union of 1707 which created the United Kingdom. There was a similar growth of national sentiment in Wales. For many decades, UK was highly centralized. In the last thirty years, there has been devolution to the regions—Wales, Northern Ireland and Scotland—in reaction to nationalist sentiments. There are nationalist movements of the Basques and the Catalans who are presently parts of Spain and would like to be independent. These are broadly left movements. It is the politics of nationalism we must look at.

The Politics of Nationalism

The LO treats nationalism as a sort of infectious disease, long eliminated from the civilized progressive world it inhabits. Thus, the arrival of Trump or the victory of Brexit has brought anguished worries of the return of the dreaded disease. Although it is global in one way, the cultural geography of the LO is West European, and includes USA and the White Commonwealth—Canada, Australia and New Zealand—within this cultural geography. There are small elite intellectual outposts around the world, but the heart is New York/London and its language is English.

Once you leave North America and Europe, nationalism is seen as a dynamic force everywhere. Most often, it has been positive in its effects, but nationalism as a dynamic force can also be destabilizing. The dialectics of nationalism are fascinating. The ways in which nationalism can turn from a positive to a negative force, or vice versa, have shaped history in contemporary times.

For postcolonial countries, nationalism is the glue that binds their country together. One cannot denigrate nationalism in India or Nigeria or Mexico. Countries encourage and indeed gain by inculcating a national consciousness, which can lead to a unity of purpose. Many postcolonial countries were created by their European imperial masters, not out of any logic of homogeneity but by drawing arbitrary lines on a map. This has certainly been the case in sub-Saharan Africa and the Middle East. In these 'composite' countries, nationalism is often the ideology which holds the diverse communities together as a single nation.

Yugoslavia is a pertinent example of the complexity of nationalism on the peripheries of Europe. As I described earlier, it was created by merging various territories of the former Ottoman Empire into a kingdom after the First World War. Serbs, Croats, Bosnians and Macedonians were thrown together. After the Second World War, it became a socialist country. But as socialism unravelled across Eastern Europe in the 1990s, instead of regarding themselves as Yugoslavs, various people began to assert themselves as Serbians or Bosnians or Croats. The break-up took a vicious turn as old nationalist antagonisms among the Slavs were revived. The Bosnian Muslims became more aware of their distinctive identity. The composite identity of Yugoslavs was a fragile creation which could not hold the diverse identities together.

As it unravelled, different groups within the overall Slav cover asserted their separateness. A community is defined not by who you include, but by setting the boundary at who you exclude. Being a Serb means not just being a Slav, but not being Croat, Bosnian, Macedonian or Slovene. Nations are based on identities built on a perceived common history and a feeling of community. The LO aspires for global brotherhood. It is a worthy ideal which says no one is excluded. That does not satisfy the many who want a tightly defined community they can identify with.

Yet, many nations are based on the accident of territory and history. Europe is a large continent and was an empire of the Romans, but over time the differences of ethnicity, language and history broke up Europe into separate territories—first as kingdoms and then as nations. USA is another accident of history and territory which was created over decades by immigrants, voluntary and captive, who wrested the land from the original occupants. America thought of itself for most of its history of the last five hundred years as a white Christian country—white Anglo-Saxon Protestant to begin with, and then white Protestant as other nationals of Europe arrived. The melting pot admitted Catholics from Ireland and later Southern Europe and South America.

When I reached America as a student in 1961, the Americans perceived themselves as a white Christian country. John Kennedy, who had just become president, had faced anti-Catholic and anti-Irish prejudices. Civil rights were yet to register their presence. The history books I read to prepare myself for my life in America were all about the American Revolution, the Constitution, and the Democracy—a history of White America written by White Americans. Even the Civil War or the War Between the States, as it would be called by politicians speaking on public platforms, was described as an all-white affair. The issue in the Civil War, everyone insisted, was the union, not slavery.

The admission of Black Americans to full citizenship began during the 1960s and one could say it is still an ongoing process. There are still states where voting rights of Black Americans are precarious. There has been a growth of Hispanics and Asians during these fifty years. There are also attempts to rewrite American history, acknowledging the contribution of Black Americans. (The integration of the gender dimension is a wholly separate and fraught issue.) Yet one could say that Native Americans have not been given their proper place in American history, as, for example, the Australians have done with their indigenous people.

In 1900, America had 76 million people, 88 per cent white of whom 0.5 million were Hispanic and 8.8 million black. By 2016, the population was 325.1 million, of whom 77.7 per cent are white, 62.6 per cent non-Hispanic and 15.1 per cent Hispanic. Thus, it is the 'European Whites' who have shrunk in proportion relative to the Hispanic Whites. The black population has remained around low double digits—it was 14.3 per cent in 2015.

The question of the colour of America as a nation is not an academic one. Barack Obama's election as the president broke a ceiling, but he was never able to escape the virulent racial prejudice that black politicians face. The sense of white entitlement was hurt. A lot of negativity which Obama faced from the Congress was no doubt tinged with that offended sense of entitlement. The election of Trump has brought up the debate about the white working class and whether movements such as Alt-Right represent white nationalism. Two hundred and forty years after 1776, America remains a divided nation. Or perhaps one should say that it is nation of nations—

White, Black, Brown, Red, Christian, Judaic, Muslim and Hindu.

These nations arrived at different times during the last five hundred years. Many faced virulent prejudice when they arrived—the Irish or the Italians and, most recently, the Muslims. There was the Chinese Exclusion Act of 1882 which mandated a ten-year moratorium on the entry of the Chinese into USA, and that was not relaxed till 1943. There was the Immigration Act of 1917 which barred all immigration from Asia. Other laws were passed restricting immigration to a small percentage of the population of each country already settled in USA. The percentage was three in 1921, and reduced to two in 1924. Although it was generally known that Jews were in dire trouble in Germany during the 1930s, there was a strict ban on their immigration. It was only after 1945 that Jews from Europe could migrate to USA. Trump's dislike of Muslims is not as 'un-American' as his critics claim. It is as American as apple pie.

USA had open borders but delayed entry of many, mostly white, immigrants into full citizenship. As the economic opportunities were plenty, people from diverse nations were attracted and they were eventually absorbed. Land was plenty, and the frontier was not closed till the late nineteenth century. Cities then became the new free pastures where people could crowd in. As they prospered, they moved into the suburbs.

The one exception is the oldest and the least voluntary immigrant group—the Black African slaves arriving to work in the vast lands growing cotton and tobacco. There was a movement after the Civil War and the abolition of slavery to encourage the outmigration of Black Americans to Africa. Abraham Lincoln was in favour of such schemes. The message for the Black American seemed to be—'Slave he was welcome, but free he had to leave America.' Despite the vast empty tracts of land to the west, Black Americans could not be settled there. They had to be sent away if they were no longer slaves. Luckily, it did not come to much. Black Americans remained, but were not treated well. Their economic betterment and citizenship rights remain, even now, short of the American promise. This is, however, not a problem Trump has created, nor one that he will solve. Nor would it have been solved by Hillary Clinton had she won, as successive presidents since John Kennedy have failed in this respect. As Condoleezza Rice has said, 'Slavery is a birthmark of America.'

Trump is also unusual in having come to power by playing on America's loss of power and status rather than the triumphal mood which had prevailed over the fifty years since John Kennedy. There was never any doubt in the past that USA was the most powerful nation. The challenges it faced—missile gap or the space race—were surmountable. Donald Trump starts with the slogan 'Make America Great Again'. This implies that USA has slipped from its position at the top. It has lost its pre-eminence for reasons unstated, but implicitly due to the two terms of a non-white president.

The proximate causes of the 'decline' are listed by Trump as uncontrolled immigration from Mexico and the loss in trade with Mexico (lately even Canada) due to NAFTA and China. Trump's inaugural address was full of negative images—of factories closed, drugs, crime and violence on the rise, or 'carnage' on America's streets. Thus, according to Trump, USA has an external as well as an internal deficit, which are the challenges he has to overcome.

The novelty of the present is that sections of the white population, which had previously partaken of the American dream, feel deprived and denied of what they consider are their rightful entitlements. The failure may have been due to non-competitive industries, a failure of the education system to equip them with marketable skills or due to lack of re-skilling facilities when their original skills were no longer in demand. This is where the economics and politics of nationalism come together. The sense of deprivation of some sections of the historically dominant community—the so-called white working class—is the fulcrum on which Trump's policies will be based.

The National Question in India

There is an uncanny similarity in this respect between USA and India. India is an old society, and one of the oldest cultures in the world, but a new nation state, created only seventy years ago. It is a territory as large as Europe, excluding European Russia. It is referred to as a subcontinent. Unlike China, another old culture and a continental territory but also the oldest continuous polity, India was never under single rule. There were various empires at times over the centuries, but none ruled over the entire subcontinent. India was divided into several large and small kingdoms frequently at war with each other. Somewhat like USA but millennia earlier, India attracted migrant groups, some arriving seeking land and livelihood while others came as marauding armies. These groups have been identified as the Shakas, Huns, Scythians and Yavanas (Ionians).

Towards the end of the first millennium CE, Muslim armies from West Asia began to invade India. They were mainly confined to North India. By the thirteenth century, they had established a commanding presence in North India with Delhi as the capital. The Delhi Sultanate, as it is called, was a succession of Afghan dynasties which ruled over North India. The Afghans were replaced by the Mughals who came from Central Asian roots of Genghis Khan and Taimur (Tamerlane). The Mughals ruled over India from the mid-sixteenth century till the end of the seventeenth. They then lingered for the next 150 years as weak occupants of the imperial throne but with little power.

In the vacuum left by the decay of Mughal power, the British emerged as rulers. The East India Company which had arrived to trade in 1600 and learnt to beseech various emperors for rights to trade began to exploit differences between local kings. There were other European trading companies, especially the French. The British defeated the French and became the dominant Western power in India. Between 1757 and 1847, they conquered most of India. They faced a massive revolt in 1857, which led to the East India Company being replaced by the British Crown. Ninety years later, the British left India.

The British had introduced Western education through the English language. Ideas of modernity were percolating through the old society, beginning from the port cities of Calcutta, Bombay and Madras* and then into the interior. There was soon the idea of India as a nation and then, obviously, of self-rule. Yet, given the diversity of the country in terms of languages and religions, and given the lack of a previous unitary state, the nationalists faced the challenge of building a narrative. One narrative was the age-old Hindu society and culture which could be said to define the nation. In the nineteenth century, faced with criticism of Christian missionaries about Hinduism, religious reform movements began to

---

*Now Kolkata, Mumbai and Chennai, respectively.

purify their religion of dubious practices and superstitions. Social reform movements wanted to modernize the society by raising the status of women, especially widows, fighting child marriage and, of course, the practice of untouchability, which was enjoined as the required behaviour on upper-caste people. There was tension between the religious revival movements and the social reform ones.

Hindus took more readily to Western education than Muslims did. As a community, the Muslims had the notion of having been the rulers of India most recently and having been displaced by the British. They had religious revival movements, but not social reform ones. Muslims missed out on the initial opening up of career opportunities to Indians in the colonial government. An attempt was made towards the last decades of the nineteenth century to introduce Western education to Muslims by the foundation of the Anglo-Oriental College in Aligarh.

In 1885, the Western-educated elite founded the Indian National Congress (INC). It began as a loyal, moderate organization—literally a coming together, a congress of diverse interests. They presented their 'demands' always as requests. They wanted to be able to compete for the Indian Civil Service, the preserve hitherto of white British. They asked for tariff protection for their nascent industries, and relief for the peasantry oppressed by high revenue demands. There was a modicum of accommodation of these demands.

As the nineteenth century gave way to the twentieth and the First World War required India's cooperation in terms of men and material, there were further constitutional concessions. Congress became a political party which Mahatma Gandhi organized into a mass movement. He launched an ecumenical Hindu–Muslim movement to protest against the likely British removal of the caliph in 1921, as I had described earlier. The movement was the largest the British had faced till then in India. But then Gandhi unilaterally suspended the movement, fearing an upsurge of violence. The Muslims felt disheartened. There was never a united Hindu–Muslim movement again after that.

As talks and negotiations proceeded on the future shape of a government in India, Muslims realized that as a minority they may be constantly outvoted in a democratic independent India. The idea of two nations within India was articulated by Muslim intellectuals. Each nation—Hindu and Muslim—had to have its own territory. A nation had to become a nation state. Congress resisted this and insisted that India should comprise both nations into one. This said, the bulk of its leadership was high-caste Hindu. There was the Hindu nationalist party, Hindu Mahasabha (Hindu Congress), which was junior to the Congress. Its leaders were less likely to defy the British and suffer imprisonment as Congress leaders did. They wanted the two-nation logic to be carried through to independence.

Before 1947, India comprised British India, which was split into provinces, many large enough to be countries on their own. Four provinces in the north-west had a Muslim majority. The largest of these four states, Punjab had 52 per cent to 48 per cent Muslim majority. In the east, Bengal also had a Muslim majority, but just 53 per cent to 47 per cent. The Muslim League demanded that a Muslim nation be set up, separate from India at independence, comprising the Muslim-majority provinces. This demand was conceded almost at the last moment, ten weeks before India gained independence. Punjab and Bengal were divided into Muslim and non-Muslim areas. Thus, East Punjab came to India as did West Bengal. The problem was that the Muslim-majority provinces were sparsely populated, except for

Bengal. The majority of Muslims lived in Hindu-majority provinces. Thus, while Pakistan was overwhelmingly a Muslim country, India at independence had a large Muslim population, a fifth of the total population, one of the largest in the world.

Partition was accompanied by the largest movement of people across the borders—Muslims moving westwards in Punjab, while Hindus and Sikhs moved eastwards. In Bengal, Muslims went eastwards and Hindus westwards. Eighteen million people moved within six months with an estimate of a loss of two million lives.

The two nation states set up at independence—India and Pakistan—have lived in a sort of cold war with each other with conflict flaring up now and again. But in India, from the beginning, another issue was raised. If there were two nations within pre-independence India and one of them—the Muslim nation—became Pakistan, why was India not a Hindu state?

Congress, which emerged as the largest ruling party, was committed to a secular view of democracy and regarded Muslims as much entitled to citizenship of India as Hindus and all other communities—Sikhs, Christians, Zoroastrians, etc. Jawaharlal Nehru, the first and longest-serving prime minister, was a Westernized modernist and sceptical about religion. He insisted that India would be a liberal, tolerant democracy, protecting the rights of minorities.

The idea of a Hindu India went underground. The party which espoused it—Bharatiya Jana Sangh (Indian People's Union)—was an offshoot of the Hindu Mahasabha. The party remained a minority movement while Congress was powerful. Nehru led India as the prime minister for seventeen years and his daughter, Indira Gandhi, for another fourteen years. It was during a crisis in her second term as prime minister that she imposed the Emergency, imprisoning all opposition party leaders, including the Jan Sangha leaders. That made them into martyrs. When the Emergency ended and new elections were called, Indira Gandhi lost. For the first time, thirty years after independence, a coalition of non-Congress parties came to power.

The Jana Sangh was at last able to overcome the stigma that their party had not gone to prison fighting for independence. They made themselves into heroes of the battle against dictatorship. The party changed its name into Bharatiya Janata Party (BJP). Congress came back to power within three years and ruled for nine more. In 1989, the Congress lost its majority. This meant also an erosion of the hegemony of Congress ideology. The idea of India as a secular, multi-religious and tolerant democracy was under attack. A sixteenth-century mosque in Ayodhya was alleged to be built on land sacred to Hindus. A mob incited by groups with close ties to the BJP destroyed the mosque in December 1992. The local state government was run by the BJP and offered no protection to the old building. Violent riots followed between Hindus and Muslims which spread all over India.

The issue of the nature of Indian nationhood was again to be debated. The BJP said that Congress secularism was not genuine. It only meant extra favours for Muslims, which were not matched by similar ones for Hindus. Thus, the financial help for Muslims going on Haj pilgrimage to Mecca was objected to, as nothing similar was available for Hindus going on pilgrimage. These are minor matters, but they opened up the debate on Indian nationhood.

Before the 2014 general elections, there were constant critiques of Modi, his policy in Gujarat and his association with the RSS.

The print media and much of television too were against him. But he had a devoted Twitter army which acted as a troll vigilante group, attacking anyone who attacked Modi. This was a novel experience for print and TV media who had not experienced such online criticism. The old hegemonic order is under attack. It is fighting back. But Modi's ascendancy will strengthen with time and especially if he is re-elected in 2019, which looks very likely.

There are other similarities between Trump and Modi in the way the national question is posed. Trump has attracted members of the majority community—European White—who feel disenfranchised. They fear they will lose their entitlements to run the country as a white country. USA is, of course, not an exclusively white country, but within living memory it has thought of itself as such. The whites complain of the Black Americans and Asians as 'line-cutters', as I mentioned earlier. The complaint of some Hindus against Muslims in India is similar. The issue here is not whether they are factually right, but whether they feel they have a grudge. The reasons for a feeling of deprivation may not be communal/racial but economic. Among groups who feel deprived, especially if they were brought up to believe that the country is theirs, resentment is likely. How a politician deals with such grievances is the interesting part.

Pollsters, opinion makers and editorialists were near unanimous that Trump had no chance. The same was true of Modi. In both cases, the presumed bias of the media was pretending to be scientific prediction. This is a variant of 'fake news'. What it really indicates is that the hegemony of the LO is facing a challenge. Whether this challenge is a serious one which will undermine the LO, or just a passing phase, remains to be seen.

FIVE

THE RESURGENCE OF ASIA

Asia is the name Europeans made up to signify what is beyond Europe in the vast Eurasian landmass. It is a negative label, land beyond the scope of European civilization. But Asia has been there sustaining great cultures across vast territories for millennia. All major religions are of Asian origin. China, India and Iran are three of the oldest continuous civilizations, each different from the other. Yet they decayed and declined during the latter half of the second millennium CE. One important shift during the third millennium CE is the return of Asia to the global stage.

Around 1500 CE, Asian countries, China and India especially, were the most prosperous in the world. Their share of world output matched their share of world population. Of course, that only meant that their per capita income was in line with the global level. It was their large population which gave them the wealth envied by the rest of the world. This wealth was very unequally distributed; so we have travellers' accounts of prosperous cities like Golconda which was the most famous, yet the peasantry was very poor and badly exploited.

China saw itself as Middle Earth, the supreme power ruling 'All under Heaven'. China exerted some sovereignty over other East and South East Asian countries within its sphere of influence.

The English sent Viscount George Macartney to establish mutual relations. Macartney had carried gifts laden in two ships of the East India Company which arrived at Tianjin and then were conveyed to where the imperial court was held in eighty-five wagons and thirty-nine handcarts, using two horses and 2,495 porters. On the morning of 14 September 1793, he presented himself and genuflected (did not kowtow, he claimed) before the emperor. He had dressed carefully for the occasion to impress the emperor. Even so, his request for a permanent relationship between the two nations was refused by the Chinese. The Chinese treated the envoy as from yet another vassal country they had not heard of before. Any notion of relations on a basis of equality or reciprocity was foreign to the Chinese.

A century earlier, the English had better luck in India. The Mughal Emperor Jahangir was the great-grandson of Babur, the founder of the Mughal dynasty, and the son of Akbar who extended the empire. Sir Thomas Roe visited Jahangir in 1615 to ask for protection for English trading factories (warehouses) in Surat, a port on the west coast of India. He was well received and stayed on for three years. The East India Company was allowed to trade.

Once the First Industrial Revolution occurred in Great Britain in the second half of the eighteenth century, a gap opened up between labour productivity in Britain and the rest of the world. As other Western countries industrialized, Asia and Africa fell behind. Coinciding with the advent of the Industrial Revolution was the conquest of India by the East India Company. This allowed the British to use Indian soldiers in thousands (financed by taxation on the Indian peasants) to extend control over Asia. Within fifty years of treating Macartney with condescension, China faced its first defeat in a war with British forces (the army comprised Indian soldiers too) in the Opium War (1839–42). China never recovered from this defeat. It had to concede extraterritorial rights in some of its ports to various Western powers. The Portuguese had started the eastward journey for spices and established their rule over parts of India and then Malacca and farther east. France and Britain and the Netherlands followed soon after. The West was the imperial power over most of the East for 150 years from the mid-eighteenth century onwards and the empires did not perish till the end of the twentieth century when Great Britain gave up its possession of Hong Kong in 1997.

Asia Enters World History

At the start of the twentieth century, Asia gave notice to Europe that it was re-entering history. Japan defeated Russia in 1905. Japan had been forced into reforming itself out of its old ways by the visit of Commodore Matthew Perry in 1854. He is credited with having 'opened up' Japan. Like all legends, this is only partially true. The Japanese had been noticing the progress the West had made from the Dutch and Portuguese ships which had arrived at their shores. Japan's modernization began during the second half of the nineteenth century with the restoration of the Meiji Empire.

Japanese modernization was built on an elite militaristic model. The feudal elements were retrained and harnessed as vanguard for modernization and Westernization. Japan did not take either the Anglo-Saxon or the French route of political democracy. It modernized in terms of mastering the Western industrial technology, but did not adopt the logic of modernity or any of the liberal values such as freedom of speech or thought. Homogeneity of the ethnic group and a single language helped cement national unity. Conformity and loyalty to the emperor were used as the glue to bind the nation together and force it to modernize.

It was the militarization which scored in the defeat of Russia. This should have been no surprise. The Romanov Empire was large but unorganized, cruel, ineffective and a laggard in terms of industrialization. It was Western arrogance that was hurt when an Asian nation defeated a Western nation. But in Asia, especially in the British colonies of India and Malaya, the French colonies in Indo-China, the Dutch colony of Netherlands East Indies (Indonesia as it became after independence) and Portuguese colonies, there was jubilation that Asia had defeated Europe.

Japan went on to impress the world with its modernization and progress. It modelled itself consciously on Western imperial powers. It aspired to and actually became the first Asian nation to be a modern imperial power. It colonized Korea in the 1890s. It gave notice to China, the big Asian power until then, that its supremacy would be challenged by Japan.

During the first half of the twentieth century, Japan began to spread its wings. It fought during the First World War on the side of the Allies. It was during the interwar period as Europe and

America were going through the Great Depression that Japan began its programme to become an Asian empire. The rise of fascism in Europe with its militaristic features had been anticipated by Japan. But Japanese fascism was not mass oriented. It came from above. Loyalty to the emperor was the cementing factor, and the military elite ran the empire on non-democratic lines.

Japanese capitalism also did not follow the liberal model. Large business houses were able to conduct their affairs in an oligopolistic way with state support. The insistence on competition or antitrust movement which was powerful in the Anglo-Saxon countries did not find any following in Japan. There was a close nexus between political and economic power as each involved a small number of leaders. Between 1860 and 1910, its industrial output trebled.

Between 1931 and 1944, Japan came close to throwing the Western powers out of Asia and becoming the sole Asian imperial power. Indeed, if the military leadership had not overreached itself and attacked Pearl Harbor, thus bringing America into the war (much to the relief of Winston Churchill and the British Empire), Japan could have emerged undefeated. It had conquered China, driven France out of Indo-China, overrun Thailand, Indonesia and Malaya. When Singapore fell in February 1942, the British were surprised. From there, Japan proceeded up the Irrawaddy to capture Burma and entered India in March 1944. It was defeated at Kohima in one of the biggest land battles of the Second World War. Indian troops led by British officers fought the Japanese who also had with them the Indian National Army made up of Indian soldiers who had surrendered when Singapore fell.

Within six months of the defeat at Kohima, Japan was bombed into surrender and forced into Americanization. Japan took advantage of its American protective umbrella to improve its image. It was a racist culture in the decades before 1945 and its excessive cruelty in China is still not forgotten by the Chinese. But it developed its image as a peace-loving artistic culture. Japan's military past remains a contentious topic within Japan as well as in East Asia.

Despite its defeat, admiration for Japanese economic achievement was not diminished in Asia. It had demonstrated that an Asian country could become like any European country in terms of economic and military power. It could avoid the liberal democratic embrace (the name of its dominant single party notwithstanding), maintain its 'Asian values' and be there at the top with the Western powers. Japan became the model Asian country to follow. Parallel with the rise of the LO in the West is the rise of Asia as an economic superpower, following a distinct non-liberal path.

The Americans wanted to make sure Japan would never again be an industrial power. But the Korean War helped Japan. It was used by the American army as a jumping-off point and a logistic base and soon began to develop. Between 1950 and 1990, Japan from a war-torn economy became one of the G7 countries. It registered double-digit growth rate between 1958 and 1973, its GDP growing fourfold. This was truly a miraculous growth achievement. After 1973, the economy slowed down to grow at 5 per cent per annum until 1990. The yen appreciated so much that in the 1980s Japan had higher per capita income than USA. There was an asset bubble which burst in the 1990s and Japan has been in a situation of high income level/low growth. As its population is declining, per capita income is still rising.

Japan was taken as a model by the 'Asian Tigers'—South Korea, Taiwan, Hong Kong and Singapore. South Korea, despite its humiliation as a colony of Japan, closely imitated Japan. If Japan had the zaibatsu, the Koreans had the chaebol.*

Rapid growth was managed by fostering a creative nexus between the government and business to have a fast trajectory during the period 1970–2010. South Korea's GDP grew at 8 per cent from 1962 to 1989, while the manufacturing output grew at 14.5 per cent over the same period. It relied on an export growth strategy to attain its status as a highly industrialized country. Subsidies were given to firms which met export targets.

In politics, South Korea has also tried its own version of the Japanese model. It has alternated between military rule and democracy; like Japan there is an Asian model in politics as much as in economics. Syngman Rhee, an authoritarian leader, was the first president after the Korean War. He was removed from power as a result of student protests in 1960. After a short democratic interlude, Major General Park Chung-hee seized power following a military coup. He legitimized himself in 1963 by founding the Democratic Republican Party and ruled for eighteen years between 1961 and 1979 till he was assassinated. The party he founded is now called the Grand Old Party of South Korea in an echo of the US Republican Party.

The dictatorship of Park Chung-hee coincided with the period of maximum rapid growth. There was a unity of purpose across the nation which was created and sustained by a patriotic fervour. Once again, a homogeneous population in terms of its ethnicity and a single language helped enormously. South Korea's per capita income was

---

*Zaibatsu is a Japanese term referring to industrial and financial business conglomerates in the Empire of Japan. Chaebol is a term applied for a South Korean form of business conglomerate.

40 per cent, below that of India, in 1960. Today, it is twenty times as much. It is the eleventh largest economy in the world. For an agrarian, backward country devastated by a war to emerge as one of the richest countries in the world is an unprecedented achievement.

Singapore is another miracle economy. As a small island, it was thought to have not much of a future when it broke from its union with Malaya in 1965. But between 1961 and 2015, it achieved a growth rate of 7.51 per cent. Lee Kuan Yew, the charismatic leader of Singapore, emphasized on discipline and tolerated no dissent. While Singapore is a democracy, there has been a single-party dominance by the People's Action Party (PAP). Lee Kuan Yew extolled Asian values of order and obedience and rejected the liberal democratic model. The success of Singapore, the only island state in the world, has been phenomenal in economic terms—the per capita income was $56,000, comparable to the richest countries. Also, unlike Japan and South Korea, Singapore has a multiracial population of Malays, Chinese and Indians.

China is the fourth miracle economy in this list. China, since the successful Communist Revolution which established the People's Republic of China (PRC) in 1949, has had a unique trajectory. As a communist nation, it departed from the Leninist model of a workers' revolutionary movement led by a communist party. In China, there was a peasants' revolution led by middle-class intellectuals who had joined the communist party. The CPC also had a long apprenticeship, lasting almost twenty years while it waited in Yenan in North China running its own peasant economy. Unlike the Russian Bolsheviks who had no experience of governing even a municipality when they came to power, the CPC had learnt to initiate policies which would enlist the support of the peasantry.

After winning power, the PRC relied on the Soviet Union for economic help. But even as a fledgling communist nation, it demonstrated its power by stopping the American troops from capturing North Korean territory. For a poor, recently pacified country to take on the most powerful military and hold it to a draw gave notice that China would make a difference. Mao was vastly ambitious for China. He wanted China to surpass the Western industrialized nation within a generation. He quarrelled with the Soviet Union which withdrew all its aid. From then on, China carried on a battle against both sides in the Cold War. The Great Leap Forward was launched on very unrealistic expectations. There was immense economic damage from trying to industrialize too fast and a most severe famine claiming forty million lives was the result. Mao retained power. But his economic policies continued to be growth retarding. Even so, China became the fifth nuclear power in the 1960s.

China wasted thirty years after 1949 experimenting with a non-capitalist economic framework.

Notwithstanding the economic ruin and political chaos, somewhat like the Soviet Union, the military was made strong even in the midst of poverty. China became a nuclear power around the time of its famine. It was a first-rate military power though a poor, underdeveloped country.

Mao succeeded in bringing USA to his door. While Nixon and Kissinger described it as bringing China into the modern world, it was in fact an acknowledgement that for the second time in twenty-five years China had held out against American military power. Vietnam had been the triumph for its National Liberation Front but China had been there to help. Asians saw it as the second defeat for the Americans in Asia with China on the winning side both times. This is, of course, not how the LO remembers the 'opening out' to China.

Yet again, the Japanese export-led model was followed by China but with a much greater role for state enterprises and only subsequent development of large private corporations (in the 'new' economy). While Deng heralded the change in 1978, the economy really took off only in 1990, ironically the year after the Tiananmen Square uprising. The Chinese opened their economy up, received foreign direct investment (FDI), and saved more than most other countries. It also managed to keep wages low by letting rural Chinese migrate in large numbers. But they were kept in constant insecurity by being denied basic access to health and housing facilities by not being issued urban living permits. Low wages meant high profits for the state corporations which saved them for investment. From 1990 till 2015, with a slight glitch around 2008–10, the Chinese growth trajectory is very similar to that of Japan and South Korea.

The miracle of the Chinese experiment is the unlikely combination of a communist polity and a capitalist economy. Chinese capitalism is of the mixed economy variety which was popular in many Third World countries in the 1950s. It is unlike the Soviet model. The Soviet Union was born in an atmosphere of blockades and rejection by the European powers. It based its economy on isolation and autarky. It inherited this notion from the German economy in wartime which was called war socialism. Lenin called it state capitalism and copied it for his revolutionary regime. Any reliance on foreign trade and benefiting from international division of labour was spurned. Hence, while it had a powerful military–industrial complex, the Soviet economy stagnated and failed to innovate in consumer goods or even capital goods.

China followed the Soviet path under Mao but once he had gone, Deng changed the course. Unlike other socialist economies, China welcomed foreign capital as well as foreign technology. The example of Taiwan and the speed with which it industrialized and became an Asian Tiger could not have been lost on Deng. While the usual Leninist prediction was of a capitalist country becoming socialist after a revolution, China reversed the course. A fully socialist economy unwound itself to create private fortunes and a homemade capitalism. There is a lot of decentralization even in the state-owned sector in China. China has thus far successfully managed this trick of moving to capitalism gradually but without relaxing the monopoly of the Communist Party on the political process. The usual idea in the LO is that increasing prosperity creates a middle class, which in turn demands and wins democratic freedoms. It is a sort of crude economism, an ersatz Marxism. The idea is that economics drives politics. Capitalist development brings forth democratic politics; it is of course a very crude simplification of the history of the last three hundred years. It has not yet been seen in China. It is unique in many respects for that reason alone.*

The four major Asian miracles in the post-war period—Japan, South Korea, Singapore and China—have a similar trajectory. The basic model is Japanese. This involves financial repression which encourages families to save but pays a low interest rate on savings. These savings are handed over to a small group of entrepreneurs

---

*Will Hutton and Meghnad Desai. 2007. 'Does the Future Really Belong to China?', *Prospect Magazine*, January; https://www.prospectmagazine.co.uk/magazine/doesthefuturereallybelongtochina, accessed 13 June 2017.

at subsidized rates.* They in turn invest and innovate and export their output. Since the markets in developed countries were open to Japan after the multilateral tariff cuts negotiated at successive GATT rounds in the post-war period, Japan was able to export manufactures and be a pioneer in the electronics sector. The zaibatsu were reborn as Sony, Mitsui, Mitsubishi and a few others that thrived under the direction of the Ministry of Trade and Industry (MITI). This was a distinctly non-Western model of capitalism. Between 1960 and 1990, Japan had a steeply rising curve for its GDP. After 1990, it levels off and the growth rate declines. Japan is a rich country. It has reached a high income plateau. It has reached, what was called in the works of Adam Smith and David Ricardo, the 'classical stationary state'. The rate of profit reaches a low level, almost zero, at which net investment ceases. Japan is a prosperous, ageing society with no great appetite for fast growth. It has got to this peak before any Western economy.

All Asian miracles have been export dependent. They were based on the assumption of continued prosperity in Western economies. But 2008 was a structural shift, and it will be a long time before Western economies resume their previous growth path. The Japanese economy had slowed down long before that. The South Korean economy, which was already exhibiting signs of maturity, and more so the Chinese economy, can no longer rely on foreign markets.

Asia has thus produced a positive challenge to the LO. It has shown in a variety of political arrangements that economic success does not require liberal democracy. This has been done by developing a dominant party democracy as in Japan and South Korea or a

---

*In China's case, these were regions or factories.

theocratic democracy as in Iran. China is also the most successful communist-ruled country in its economy, its military capability and its unique politics. It also has a vaulting ambition to re-emerge as Middle Earth.

A New Global Order?

It is China which will issue the challenge of an alternative to the LO. It has to rethink the Japanese model. It is shifting to domestic demand. Unlike Japan, it has, for the time being, good demographics, though its population will be ageing soon. There are still fifteen more years with a growing population which China can use to shift to a domestic demand-based growth model. China achieved another milestone last year when its currency, the renminbi (yuan), was included in the Standard Drawing Right (SDR), a composite currency issued by the IMF. Thus, now Asia has two SDR currencies—yen and yuan—while the West has the dollar, the sterling and the euro.

The IMF and the World Bank were set up at Bretton Woods in 1944, anticipating the victory of the Allies. Their governance is monopolized by the Western powers. The president of the World Bank is always an American and the managing director of the IMF a European. Efforts to change these arrangements have not met with much success. During the Asian crisis of 1997 (discussed in Chapter 1), Asian countries felt that the IMF was biased against them. China has taken advantage of its large foreign exchange reserves—$4 trillion at its highest—to establish rival lending banks to help the countries neglected by the Bretton Woods institutions. The Asian Infrastructure Investment Bank (AIIB) has been set up to give development loans to countries in the Asia-Pacific region. The second bank, called the New Development Bank, has been set up jointly with other BRICS nations—Brazil, Russia, India, China and South Africa.

China is more ambitious than Japan to become a global leader as an alternative to Western, especially the US, leadership. It has a dream to become the Middle Kingdom once again. It has launched the One Belt One Road (OBOR) programme. This ambitious infrastructure programme aims to connect China with all of Eurasia. Reviving the old Silk Road, China has launched the Silk Road Economic Belt (SREB) which would connect by rail and road all the countries along the Eurasian landmass, such as the North Belt which would be a train going from Beijing to London. There are also the central and the southern SREBs. The Central Belt goes through Central Asia and then via the Middle East to Southern Europe. The south SREB takes in South East and South Asia. This is an addition to the classic Silk Road. Countries along the Silk Road are also members of the AIIB. Thus, investments can be coordinated with the logic of the SREB. In addition, there is the twenty-first-century Maritime Silk Road (MSR). This is a chain of seaports down the South China Sea and via the Indian Ocean into the Mediterranean.

No previous great power, except perhaps Rome, has ever displayed such ambition to link distant parts of the world in a single network. The maritime empires, Great Britain especially, did maintain and police the seaways for trade. But the dream of a railroad spanning Africa from Cairo to the Cape never materialized. Since 1945, USA has taken up the maritime security responsibility. But to try several ambitious projects is a unique Chinese ambition.

Indian Exceptionalism

It is India, the second most populous country and the other strong economy with China since 1500 CE, which is the exception. Their combined share of world income matched their share of world population. The Asian resurgence or the Japanese model is all about East Asia and South East Asia. No such miracle growth path is seen west of the Mekong. India has grown only lately since 1991, having wasted forty-plus years since independence in a romantic experiment with socialist dirigisme. Its growth over the last twenty-five years has been often above 6 per cent, but not consistently so. Yet India is also an exception in being the largest liberal democracy in the world and the only one among the former colonies or the Third World to have been one continuously for seventy years.

It was the first Asian country to have a textile mill started by a native Indian in the mid-nineteenth century as well as the first railways and telegraph in Asia. Under British rule, its fledgling industrial sector grew at 8 per cent per annum, between 1860 and 1900. The First World War further boosted industrial growth. But India suffered during the interwar years as it was hitched to the British economy which was itself in a depression. Again the Second World War helped India on the industrial front. At independence, India was the seventh largest industrial nation in the world. Then, it steadily lost this position by a series of well-meaning but economically inefficient policies which froze the industrial sector at around a fifth of the economy. India made the mistake of taking the Soviet Union as its model. This was because of the high reputation the USSR had acquired as a victor in the Second World War. Its Five Year Plans were said to be the key to rapid industrialization. India, like the USSR, pursued autarky as much as it could, closing down many of the established trade links. It took a severe crisis in its balance of payments in 1991 to jolt the political classes to abandon their ruinous policies and open the economy to trade and investment.

Over the last twenty-five years (1991–2016), India has registered a high single-digit growth, not at a steady but at a variable rate. Its miracle was to take the lead in information and communication technology (ICT). While previously India had been obsessed about hardware—machines to make machines—it found its niche in software. India became the centre for Western multinationals to outsource their back-office activities, as its young trained software experts went to the headquarters of these companies to help out. India was able to leapfrog, thanks to the mobile telephony revolution. Today, it has a billion mobile phone subscribers.

While its policies of protecting jobs in the modern sector led to a stagnation of employment and output growth in the manufacturing industries, India developed a large and productive service sector. This has rebounded to its advantage. Thus it is ironic that while India has never been a miracle economy, it can teach the Asian model a thing or two. It has never been export driven, but depends on domestic demand. Its demographics are good, thanks to the failure of its family planning policy. During the 1960s, population growth was regarded as a negative factor for development. Both China and India had policies to restrict the number of children that a family should have. India had a policy of two children per couple; China a single-child policy. China's policy was a success which it now regrets. Its population would be ageing fast. India's policy failed, and it boasts of its demographic good fortune. The median age of the Indian population is twenty-six.

India is enjoying a late surge. Since the beginning of this century, it has shown the potential for sustained growth at high single-digit rates. But India being not quite an Asian Tiger, there was a let-down during 2009–14. Now with a new government led by Narendra Modi, growth has resumed but it is yet to be seen if it can be sustained even for ten years.

Is India an Asian or a European Country?

One could argue that India is somewhat out of Asia. Indians think they are part of Europe, culturally and ideologically. Once Buddhism left India, defeated by resurgent Hinduism around the end of the first millennium CE, India decoupled itself from Asia. The rest of Asia, especially East and South East Asia, were won over by Buddhism. In India, all signs of the influence of Buddhism faded. Then, a peculiar result of contact with the British enhanced the distance from Asia.

Sir William Jones, who was a judge in the East India Company's Bengal Presidency in the late eighteenth century, discovered the Indo-European family of languages. He concluded that Sanskrit, Greek, Latin and Persian shared similar words and grammatical structures. This discovery (now questioned) profoundly influenced Indian thinking. There were stories about a common Central or Northern European origin of the languages from a single Ur-language. Then it was argued that various groups of these people dispersed, some going to Western Europe, others to Persia and some to India. Termed as 'Aryans', they were the inheritors of the original culture and language. This story was much accepted till very recently when the Nazis brought the notion of Aryan culture into its current bad odour. But as late as 1935, Stanley Baldwin, the British prime minister, argued in the House of Commons how British rule in India had brought together again two branches of the original Aryans. There was a story of Aryan 'invasion' of India. It was believed that North Indians were the descendants of the Aryans while South Indians were the original tribal people who had been pushed southwards. Much of this has now been exploded as make-believe. But for Indians during the nineteenth century and later, this was an immensely influential story. There were attempts to trace the original 'home' of the Indians. A fervent India nationalist, Bal Gangadhar Tilak argued that the Aryans who came to India were from the Arctic.

The Indian elite began to think of itself as European. This elite has been educated in the West. The dominant language in government and politics was English. In the decades before independence, the direction of travel and indeed cultural influence was towards the West. The only Indian leader who visited Japan and China was Rabindranath Tagore, the great Bengali poet who was also the first Asian to win the Nobel Prize in 1913. The others—Gandhi and Nehru—were educated in England and retained a fondness for that country all their lives.

Unlike China, as I have discussed above, India had never been a single polity, under a single ruling dynasty. It was more like Europe, an area united by a common religion—Christianity in Europe and Hinduism in India. But if this idea is adopted, it runs into the problem that for almost five hundred years between the thirteenth and seventeenth centuries, North India was ruled by Muslims—Afghans, Turks and Mughals. Thus, even if India was a Hindu subcontinent, it became a multi-religious polity by the time the British moved into power during the late eighteenth and early nineteenth centuries.

At independence, as we have seen above, British India was partitioned into India and Pakistan. Pakistan was to embody the Muslim 'nation' within British India as a nation state. The question then was if Pakistan was the state for the Muslim nation, was India the state for the Hindu nation? Nehru, the head of Congress, rejected the two-nation theory. He asserted that India was a secular, multi-faith nation state. His idea was the central pillar of the idea of India for the first fifty years after independence.

The effect of the partition of the Indian subcontinent made it difficult for India to achieve the sort of single-nation consciousness which East Asian nations have. The idea of India as a secular country has been challenged by the newly dominant BJP over the years. It argues for India to be declared a Hindu nation, though accommodating Muslims and other minorities with guaranteed rights. Unlike other Asian countries, India has a very diverse population, many religions, scores of languages, and the country chose to have a British-style democracy. It has a contentious and very free style of politics. Though the slogan is 'Unity in Diversity', India has never had the single-mindedness of purpose in its seventy years of history as an independent country.

Narendra Modi has been a surprisingly successful prime minister in his term so far. The BJP is now challenging the Congress for a hegemonic position in Indian politics. Modi admires Singapore and Lee Kuan Yew. He wants India to achieve rapid growth with a unity of purpose.

India and China

As two of the oldest continuous civilizations in Asia, and indeed in the world, there is a lot of shared history between India and China. Buddhism migrated from India to China, and many Buddhist monks went from India to China and others from China came to India. Indeed, we know of some bits of India's history—such as the story of Nalanda University—thanks to the traveller's account of Schwen Zhang (Hieu-en-Tsang) who visited India in the seventh century. Tibet, which stands between the two countries, also turned Buddhist and became a place where Buddhist manuscripts and scholarship flourished.

It was, however, the modern period which sowed the seeds of what has become a major border dispute between India and China. It was during British rule that the border between India and China was drawn. The Chinese state was weak at that time, in the early years of the twentieth century. China claimed suzerainty over Tibet which was challenged by the British. The border drawn went across the range of the Himalayan mountains. The McMahon Line bore the name of the British civil servant who negotiated the treaty. The Chinese considered that line an unjust imperialist imposition.

The Indian National Congress was however friendly towards China in its policies. Chiang Kai-shek, who headed the Kuomintang (Guomindang) government, visited India during the Second World War, and he was warmly greeted during his stay. India sent a medical mission led by Dr Dwarkanath Kotnis to China during the Second Sino-Japanese War in 1938. In March 1947, on the eve of the soon-to-arrive independence, Nehru presided over an Asian Relations Conference where China was a welcome guest. When China baulked at the arrival of a Tibetan delegation, India acknowledged China's control over Tibet and the crisis was smoothed over.

After Indian independence, China opened the question of the

border. The maps were old and the terrain was unmanageable. It was not certain where the border truly was. India took the view that the borders it had inherited from the British rulers were indeed the rightful borders. China had hoped to correct what it thought was an outcome of past injustice meted by British imperialists. There were parleys between Nehru and Zhou Enlai, which raised hopes of a peaceful settlement. The two countries affirmed the Pancha Shila (Panchsheel Treaty), five principles embodying peaceful coexistence.

Chinese control over Tibet had been weak in the years before the Communist Revolution. But the PRC was a strong government and asserted its control over Tibet. It was also not respectful of the religious leadership of the Dalai Lama as its communist philosophy was anti-religious. The Dalai Lama was forced into exile from Tibet and he took asylum in India. Nehru was happy to provide asylum to him and his large party of followers. It is rumoured that India had implicit support of USA for this gesture. China's hostility to the Dalai Lama has remained unabated over the decades he has been in exile.

India discovered in the late 1950s that China had built a road in Aksai Chin in the north-east corner in the Ladakh region of Jammu and Kashmir. Nehru tried to minimize the shock, by saying that not a blade of grass grew in those parts. (During the parliamentary debate, an MP pointed to his own and Nehru's bald heads and said that just because nothing grew there did not mean the heads were dispensable!) But the Indian public was not happy. Soon there was news of incursions by China across the McMahon Line. Nehru ordered the army to remove the incursion. However, the Chinese armies were much better prepared and better equipped than the

Indian soldiers. India suffered even greater humiliation when the Chinese unilaterally withdrew behind the disputed border.

The humiliation dealt by China had a salutary effect on India. There had been dissatisfaction brewing meanwhile in the four states of South India about the domination of the North. Earlier, in the Constitution of India, a clause had been inserted stating that while English was the national language, Hindi would replace it as the language fifteen years after the Constitution came into effect with the birth of the republic in 1950. As the deadline approached, the four states of South India, whose languages have a different structure from North Indian languages as these are derived from Sanskrit, were unhappy. There were even serious talks of a 'peaceful' second partition. The debacle in 1962 however made all Indians realize that it was the territory which united them, rather than the language or religion. All talk of southern secession ceased.

The defeat by China poisoned the last years of Nehru's leadership of India. The country forgave him, but he died soon after in May 1964, a broken man. He had led the country he lived in to become a vibrant, tolerant and liberal democracy. He failed to accelerate India's growth rate or remove old social practices, such as dowry, caste divisions or untouchability. But without him, India could have submitted to the cycles of authoritarian and democratic rule like Pakistan or other Asian countries.

Successive governments in India have tried to settle the border issue peacefully while still at the same time have improved its patrolling of the border. It was not till twenty-five years after the 1962 border incursion that an Indian prime minister, Rajiv Gandhi, Nehru's grandson, visited China. Since then, the border issue has lain dormant.

In 1998, India exploded its own nuclear device and was put under sanctions by the Nuclear Suppliers Group (NSG). A few years later, Dr Manmohan Singh, the prime minister at the head of a Congress-led UPA, struck up a close diplomatic friendship with George W. Bush, the forty-third President of USA. The story goes that when George W. Bush realized that there was a second country with a population of a billion besides China his interest was aroused about India. When he met Dr Manmohan Singh, he was delighted. Bush began with a quote from the New Testament and found that Singh could match him quotation for quotation from the Gospels. They struck up a personal friendship. Bush became active in lifting the sanctions on India in the NSG. India and USA came closer together with an implicit understanding of a military alliance, just in case either needed the other.

This understanding, which led to India abandoning its non-aligned policy, is an undeclared alliance against China. Obama had endorsed this both with Dr Manmohan Singh and more recently with Narendra Modi. USA has also been active on India's behalf and tried to have India admitted to the NSG.

The India–China dispute about the border has remained a problem which flares up now and then, but never too seriously. Lately, China has raised objections to a region in the north-east corner of India, which is the state of Arunachal Pradesh, being a part of India. China's argument is that this region was included in the Indian borders only as late as 1937. It has refused to issue visas if people come from that region, and insist on stapling a separate document to the passport to indicate the provisional nature of the visa. It has also done the same with citizens of Jammu and Kashmir, again doubting India's claim on the region. In retaliation, lately, India has refused to concede the 'One China' claim and has referred to Taiwan separately, a sensitive issue with China.

It is the years since Modi became the prime minister that this low-key retaliation strategy has been used. Modi has blown hot and cold in the Sino-Indian relationship. He has courted President Xi at the same time as promising Vietnam to help with its offshore drilling problems since China asserts its claim to the South China Sea and frowns upon other nations' activities. China in retaliation has blocked India's entry into the NSG.

It is the arrival of Donald Trump with his open hostility to China on the issue of trade which can light the fuse. Trump has also changed his tune vis-à-vis China. He has been friendly with Xi since he needs him to tackle North Korea's nuclear threat against Japan and South Korea. It is early days yet, but Obama had already begun his pivot to Asia-Pacific and warned China about its expansionary activities in the South China Sea. China, of course, asserts its sovereignty in the South China Sea. It has disputes with Japan as well as the Philippines about the islands in that region.

A subsidiary element in this volatile mixture is the position of North Korea (Democratic Republic of Korea). It represents perhaps the most extreme departure from the LO and yet it has, in some sense, 'thrived'. Despite its poverty, North Korea has continued to use a Soviet-style economic model and concentrated its resources on its military–industrial complex. It has now a nuclear capability and has developed the technology of delivering nuclear missiles. It openly defied world opinion, and in March 2017 landed some missiles in Japanese maritime territory. China is supposed to keep North Korea under control, but it is not at all certain to what extent China would go to exert its influence. North Korea has been unique in having a hereditary communist dictatorship. The present incumbent, President Kim Jong-un, is the third generation of the family of Kim Il-sung who ruled over North Korea in the 1950s. The family intrigues about succession are monarchical in their violence. In February 2017, there was an alleged murder by agents of Kim Jong Nam, a stepbrother of the president, in Kuala Lumpur airport in Malaysia. North Korea may yet be the cause of an accidental nuclear war.

Asia's Challenge

Asia is Europe's Other. It lost out at the start of the 1500s but over the last hundred odd years it has been catching up with the West. It has mastered the trick of economic growth and acquired sophisticated weaponry. It has fashioned its own version of democracy and tolerance. India is the only exception to this. But many people argue that India's fascination with Western liberalism is a thin, elitist veneer on what is a distinctly Indian, indeed Hindu, culture. Modi's success in winning a majority and his achievements since 2014 have raised questions about the future of liberalism in India. As I discussed earlier, India's diversity may yet guarantee that it stays a liberal, pluralist society.

It is China which has the aspiration to restore itself to the top of the world, the Middle Kingdom as it used to be called. It has built itself an outstandingly vibrant economy and has climbed up the ranking among the G20 within thirty years of launching its growth programme. Its ambitious programme of recreating the Silk Road across Eurasia, building an alternative financial platform for global development and its aggressive stance in the South China

Sea are portents of a serious challenge to the LO. The 'endogenous' challenge to the LO which Donald Trump represents may yet clash with China to thwart its wish to build its own global order.

SIX

QUO VADIS?

Where will the world go from here? The optimistic tone of Francis Fukuyama's classic account in *The End of History and the Last Man* celebrated the peak of rational self-consciousness of humanity. Humanity had arrived at the pinnacle of a liberal, tolerant and prosperous order in which wars could be thought of as a matter of the past, where human dignity, rights and basic social equality were recognized. It was the best of all possible worlds.

But perhaps not. If at all true, it was a reality for the North Atlantic corner of West European civilization where capitalism was the dominant mode of production (to add a Marxian expression to the Hegelian discourse). Elsewhere, both in the lower income strata of the North Atlantic region itself or in the Asiatic, African and the South American worlds, history had not come to an end.

Truly speaking, the LO had not behaved humanely in its empires in Asia and Africa. USA had fought, with some allies, two long wars in Asia—in Korea and then in Vietnam and Cambodia. But by the 1990s, old empires had been reinterpreted as happy stories; the wars in Asia were forgotten. The old slaves and defeated people had come and settled in the midst of the LO territory. All cosmopolitan metropolises now enjoyed from around the world the cuisines, the music, the art and the literature. The world was your home if you lived in the LO and the world had indeed arrived at your home.

But lately there have been a few rude awakenings. First is the totally alienating confrontation with Islam. A small inkling first came through in 1979 when the rampaging mobs in Tehran besieged the American embassy on the urging of the Ayatollahs whose fatwas made no sense in the modern world but who proved as adept at the use of modern technology as at their medieval theology. It became clear that one could use modern technology expertly without endorsing modernity. The Islamic threat later spanned its wings as jihadism and Wahhabism. The terror attacks around the world, which are now frequent occurrences, remind the LO that the world is now a different place from home. When the world comes to its home, the LO realizes the danger lurking constantly elsewhere.

Then there is the Asian challenge. There is not only an alternative path to economic prosperity, which is different from what the LO favours, but China is eager to displace Western powers, especially USA from the position of the world leader that it holds by launching its Silk Road strategy.

The real shock, however, is not of 'foreign' cultures which are hostile. It is the emergence of the enemy at home—Brexit and Donald Trump, nationalism and racism, the growth of the extreme left and right political parties across Europe—which has shaken the LO. The growth of protectionism and the threats to fiscal and financial orthodoxy have added to the fear. Could the LO end? Or is the world just living through a temporary aberration after which normal service will resume?

Cheer up for a start. Consider the possibility that Donald Trump may only last one term or even get impeached before he finishes his first term. Even during his first hundred days, he proved remarkably amateurish in wielding executive power. No one seems to have told him about the separation of powers. He will probably get fed up and frustrated and walk off in a huff. But all that perhaps is just wishful thinking. Nor is there any realistic prospect that Trump would be successfully impeached by Congress. None of the previous attempts at impeachment came to a definitive conclusion. It is hardly likely that Trump can do worse than Clinton or Andrew Johnson.

Brexit may yet come to nothing if the negotiations between UK and the EU 27 end up in a bespoke deal, which would preserve the status quo ante. Perhaps parties on both sides will behave rationally and recognize their mutual dependence. The extreme political fringe may only be the result of the long recession and may pass as and when the bottom is turned and normal prosperity is restored. Elections in the Netherlands in March 2017 turned out to be much less favourable to Geert Wilders's anti-Muslim Party for Freedom. Who knows this may be a portent of the receding tides of right populism or a blip. Geert Wilders did get as many as nineteen seats, more than the Greens and as many as the Christian Democrats and the Liberal Progressives. Mark Rutte, the incumbent prime minister, got thirty-one seats, the highest for any party, but fewer than what he had. In UK, in the local municipal elections, UKIP lost all its

150-odd seats and gained only one. It did not do any better at the general election in June 2017. In France though, the established parties of the left and right lost at the first round of the presidential elections, leaving only the outsider but liberal Emmanuel Macron and Marine Le Pen as candidates for the final round. Macron won, and thus re-established the fragile hold of the LO in France. There is fragmentation, but the real cliff edge has not been reached. In UK, as new elections were called by Theresa May, it emerged that the extreme right-wing UKIP has lost all its support. If anything, unlike France, British politics has strengthened the old parties. The Conservative and Labour Parties command a higher percentage of voter support—83 per cent—than they have for thirty years. There is no clear movement against the LO here.

Extend the optimism to the possibility that like its sister religion Christianity, Islam may also experience a reformation and the medieval sectarian theologies of Wahhabism and Salafism may be rejected by Muslims themselves. Islamism has been as damaging for Muslim countries as for the rest. Daesh, the latest manifestation of Islamist jihadism, has been combated by Iraq with the help of Saudi Arabia (and the West). At the time of publication, it looked like the Iraqi army was winning the battle of capturing the headquarters of Daesh. It could be the beginning of the end of a long period of struggle against Islamist terrorism which began with 9/11.

To put one's faith in an Islamic reformation is to jump deep into the logic of the stadial theory of history, which Adam Smith and the Scottish Enlightenment bequeathed to the Europeans, and which Hegel and, later, Marx used so imaginatively. It would require us to believe that all 'civilizations' go through the same cycle sooner or later. The template prepared by European Christianity in the sixteenth century—Reformation, the Thirty Years War and the Westphalian Peace, the rise of science and modernity—will recur in the Muslim world. We are all secretly economic materialists and love the stadial theory, but it would be wise not to rely on it as an infallible guide.

Decentring

Some of the considerations mentioned earlier give some reasons for hope while others urge caution. But the more serious questions are being raised by forces which are internal to the LO, endogenous in other words. They are products of the LO but may end up undermining it. There are no certainties here either way, positive or negative. But we need to look at these forces to prepare ourselves to meet the challenges they pose.

Prominent among them is the recent development in ICT. The possibilities of blogging, tweeting and reaching out to distant contacts via Facebook have decentred the well-known process of information generation and dissemination. There was a time when respected newspapers and a few TV newscasters were held to be guides of public opinion. When I reached America in 1961, James (Scotty) Reston of *The New York Times* was a much-read and believed columnist. His column was quoted and often set the agenda on many occasions. When John Kennedy was assassinated, Columbia Broadcasting System (CBS) called Walter Cronkite to appear on air so that people would believe the tragic news. Cronkite had credibility as the truth teller. The print and electronic media had a small number of leading outlets which shaped public opinion.

Fast forward to today and newspapers are facing serious competition from a variety of sources. The economics of print media has been undermined by online access. Newspapers are losing print readership while online access is difficult to price in a way which would have profits at the end of the line. Blogs compete for news and are believed as much as previously dominant newspapers. YouTube has more watchers than TV channels. There are multiple sources, various technologies and constant innovation which have broken the solidity of the media as a pillar of the LO.

This is where the notion of fake news as against real news becomes tricky. Who is to certify that some news is fake and some genuine? The earlier trust in newspapers and channels when they were few has dissipated in the face of competition from multiple actors. As economists would say, the media had power when it was an oligopoly with a few large dominant players. Now the media has to prove its worth against many small and sometimes a few large sources. The old power has eroded. The music business has been facing a similar revolution caused by the streaming of music through a smartphone. The smartphone is getting smarter in each generation and may soon displace the stationary TV fixed on a wall at home to be gawped at by the family. Soon movies would be watched on smartphones, and big cinema houses would be empty.

This process of the established providers of news losing their command can be labelled 'decentring'. There is no longer a single source from where true news emanates. The same process led to the election of Donald Trump, as I explained earlier. It is by avoiding the centre ground and indeed realizing that the electorate is decentred that he fashioned his winning strategy.

A New Way of Doing Democracy

The ancient Athenians met in the agora—the marketplace—to conduct democratic politics. The electorate was limited—no women and no slaves, just adult men. You could get them together and address them. A Demosthenes or Pericles could move them to passionate action. This was direct democracy. The act of speaking was not just persuasive but shaping the decision to be made by the listeners—the electorate. We now have indirect democracy. Yet, the old practice of addressing the gathered multitude has survived, though the decision is not made on the spot. It was not feasible to construct a national agora when the electorate got larger as we moved from city states to larger territorial states.

Liberal democracy has always lived in fear of the mob. The demos has to be controlled and filtered through an election process which replaces the demos by its agents. The founding fathers of the American Constitution proposed an electoral college to put a distance between the mob and the president-elect. There is a tension between consulting the demos and letting it have its own way. There are ways, old and new, of consulting and controlling the demos. These ways could be transformed, indeed undermined, by technology.

Speech-making remains an important part of democratic persuasion. Even as recently as the 1970s, British politicians had to have the gift of addressing hustings—large election-related meetings. These campaign speeches still happen, but the effective mode of communication has been TV for some decades now. You no longer need to gather people in the agora. You can reach them in their living rooms. But now they can already download your speech live on their smartphones while going about their business. The agora is in cyberspace.

But then how long can our voting practices remain as they are? In UK and USA, people visit polling booths at given times and cast their votes, by filling in slips of paper or pulling some handle. In India, there are EVMs to gather and later count the votes of the 850-million-strong electorate. But why should we need to go to any specific location to cast the vote? Why not vote online, via your smartphone? Why should there be voting booths? All you need is your number on the voting register and a personalized password to vote online from anywhere at any time. Of course, with new technology comes new danger. We have to be sure that the process cannot be hacked into. Cybersecurity has been a major concern since the Russians have been suspected of hacking into the American presidential election process. Online voting would need to be made hacking proof.

Take this possibility a step further. The settled form of representation is of someone selected by a form of majority vote. In a first-past-the-post system, it is plurality which decides—the person with the largest number of votes is elected. If the contest is between just two candidates, then the winner gets a majority, but not in a multi-cornered contest. According to many people, in other fairer systems such as single transferable vote, all contestants are ranked and the lowest vote getter on first preferences is eliminated and their second preferences distributed among the rest. The elimination process continues till one person has a majority of preferences. There are proportional voting systems which cut the direct link between the voters and the candidates. People vote for parties who list their candidates in order of preferences.

All these systems are occasional and indirect. They select a representative for the constituency which is voting. That chosen person is the agent of the electorate for the term of the Parliament. But what sort of agent is the elected member? Edmund Burke, in his famous speech to the electors of Bristol, argued that he was not their delegate, but their representative. He reflected their interests as he himself deemed fit. But is that necessarily a good model of agency?

Burke was speaking at a time when the electorate was not only small but it was difficult for the electorate to contact their MP. They could have sent him a letter but that too would have taken time. But now we have many possibilities which invite a redefinition of the relationship between the electorate and the representative.

We now have the possibility of frequent and continuous consultation between the electorate and their agent, the elected member. As issues come up, they can tell the elected member which way to vote. He/she can then make his/her own calculation of where the majority of the voters are on any issue.

We could go further. Why should voters not be consulted constantly on individual issues, either by their representative or by the collectivity, such as the Parliament when it is debating and deciding an issue? Why not poll people on an issue-by-issue basis so the decision makers know the preferences of the electorate. The annual budget could be decided by polling people on taxes and expenditure decisions. One could have continuous direct democracy.

We have the technology to replace Parliaments by continuous online consultation and decision making. This would be the limit of decentred democracy. It would undermine the political elite. One would not need elected representatives. We could do it ourselves and not via agents—our MPs or congressmen and congresswomen.

There is a fear of plebiscitary democracy in liberal circles. It has been the device used by aspiring dictators in the past. Karl Marx denounced Napoleon III for using that device to seize power in France in the wake of the failure of the 1848 revolution. 'Bonapartism' is the label he attached for that tactic. But the trick of the Bonapartist is to use one vote for perpetual power. If the plebiscites were continuous, there would be a different way of doing politics.

The prospect of a continuous direct democracy is within the realm of possibility, thanks to the smartphone. The dissatisfaction with the election of Trump does not have to be endured long. One could envisage an ongoing technological arrangement for continuous direct democracy. This would be anti-elitist and totally decentring in terms of power.

A New Economy?

The LO delivered mass prosperity in the decades after 1945 by expanding manufacturing employment and enhancing labour productivity by constantly improving the capital stock used by workers. Even after the 1970s, when manufacturing went offshore to Asia, the financial revolution aided by the new ICT technology prolonged the prosperity. Of course, there were winners and losers but overall incomes went up.

The crisis of 2008 brought that process to a halt. Western economies have been going through a slowdown, a secular stagnation. Unemployment has been higher than before. Many disappointed workers have dropped out of the active labour force. Wages have stopped rising as they did in the good old days of the Keynesian quarter-century.

Capitalism has grown through successive long cycles of technological innovations since the first Industrial Revolution powered by steam. Each revolution has been based around a cluster of innovations which transformed the economy. Each cluster sets off a long cycle of around forty to fifty years which goes through a boom and then goes bust. These cycles are not regular as clockwork, but they offer us a heuristic device to think of the future. Joseph Schumpeter, the Austrian economist who coined the idea of entrepreneurs as the bold pioneers who innovated and dragged the economy along, was offering his idea as an answer to Marx who said the origin of profits was in exploitation of living labour by the owners of capital who hired the workers. Not so, Schumpeter argued. It was the richness of the science and technology base which led to inventions and the entrepreneur saw the profit possibilities of transforming the invention into an innovation. Each cycle of innovation created a new economy, but also destroyed the old economy. It was a process of creative destruction which defined capitalism.

The global economy has not had a cluster of innovations since Silicon Valley transformed ICT technology. The ramifications of that revolution are still spreading through. The biggest fortunes today are with the pioneers of Facebook, Google and Microsoft. Amazon has changed our shopping habits. But the revolution has spent its course. Productivity is not rising any longer. In a way, the crisis of 2008 announced the end of the boom phase of the long cycle inaugurated by the ICT revolution.

So when do we get the next cluster? There are telltale signs of what is coming. The driverless car has been making headlines. Tesla is known as a pioneer, though it is yet to deliver the product. Other companies are jumping into the fray and exploring the possibility of beating the early starter. There are developments in robotics and in artificial intelligence. Till now, these are seedlings yet to sprout completely but there is little doubt that the next revolution is around the corner.

For centuries, human physical effort has been the primary input. It has been aided by draught animals, tools and implements. We moved on to extensive use of fossil fuels and machinery. Over the years, workers have been supported by more and more expensive and productive machinery. We measure the possibility of economic prosperity by looking at labour productivity.

Now contemplate the possibility that instead of human labour doing work, capital will be labour as well as machinery. A driverless car eliminates human effort. Robots can replace human workers and work more efficiently, without mistakes and never falling sick or going on strike. Artificial intelligence can remove the need for even intellectual work by human beings.

For decades, we have been warned about the end of work, thanks to automation. There were warnings that we will have too much leisure. It has not come this far. But perhaps all those early warnings were not wrong, just early.

How many of us remember what the world was like before mobiles or emails? Even telephones were rare possessions outside the developed world. When I came to America, I knew that it was nearly impossible to communicate with my family back in India, even during an emergency. They did not have a telephone. Even within India, telephones between cities were difficult to manage. You could send telegrams within India or cables from America to India. But even those took their time. Now, grandparents talk to their grandchildren at the other end of the world on smartphones or iPads routinely.

Our lives have been irreversibly transformed. Now if robotics and artificial intelligence replace living labour, what will the world look like? The most urgent issue that arises is: How would people receive incomes to meet their daily expenses? Who will pay the tax to finance the welfare state? Will we need to devise a scheme of universal basic income which would entitle each and every one of us to a decent standard of living without employment? Will the money to finance this come from taxes paid by those who own and/or produce robots?

The claim of the LO to have delivered mass prosperity for the first time in the history of the world is under severe threat. There will be increasing productivity in the economic system but divorced from human effort, it will break the link between effort and reward. New rules will have to be found to gauge who gets how much since there will be no skills or effort observable in a practical way.

One may take consolation in the likelihood that such a complete change would take a long time to come. However, that would be unwise. Imaginative ways will have to be found to rethink the very nature and purpose of an economy. Is it to produce goods and services or to provide a way of giving people resources to survive and flourish? Relieved of the drudgery of economically productive work, would we be able to cultivate the finer arts of living, conversations and collective activities which we cannot indulge in at the moment? Will we find better ways of living or be bored out of our minds?

The Coming Armageddon

It may be less painful to contemplate more familiar dangers. One such possibility is of a war between America and China. Donald Trump wants to make America great again, that is, reoccupy the top position from which it is being displaced by China (or so he believes). There is, on the other hand, China which has launched a vastly ambitious programme of infrastructure development spanning the Eurasian landmass which has never been attempted before. China wants to be numero uno. There is here the classic situation of the rising power challenging the old leader. This is how Germany entered the First World War to challenge Great Britain. One could add the Cold War which was the rivalry between the top-ranking power USA and the number two USSR.

War of this kind is not inevitable, and there is always the hope that reason will prevail. But one cannot be sure. There are straws in the wind. The USA–India relationship has been evolving over the last ten years, which has all the telltale signs of a 'just-in-case' military understanding, if not alliance. India and China have been having a border dispute, as mentioned earlier. Pakistan and India have been in a cold war of their own. China has been Pakistan's ally till date.

It is, of course, not a certainty but of all the likely conflicts around the world with a global impact, a war between USA and India on the one side and China, aided by Pakistan, on the other is one that cannot be ruled out. A certain incendiary element has been added by the behaviour of North Korea and its aggressive intent towards Japan and South Korea.

It is not at all clear whether such a war will strengthen the LO or damage it seriously. It depends, of course, on who wins, if winning and losing are at all clearly definable. But there is little doubt that a victory of USA (even under Trump) and India over China and North Korea is what the liberals would cheer. But then that is not a certainty by any means.

No Certainty

Optimists have been defined as those who expect the world to get better. Pessimists on the other hand think it will continue in the usual mess. Revolutionaries have to be optimists, though the change they espouse may not make the world better. The possibilities discussed above—continuous direct democracy, elimination of human work effort, war between USA and China along with India, Pakistan, North and South Korea plus Japan—are eventually generated by optimism, the idea that the world will change. Or perhaps not. Perhaps the world will continue as before with the LO for the few and the grim reality for the many. Bad though it may sound, it is the devil we know, and though we may not admit it, love.

POSTSCRIPT

On 8 June 2017 at 10 p.m. local time, the exit poll results for the UK general election were declared. When Prime Minister Theresa May had called the election on 18 April, it was thought to be a masterstroke. The government had a slim majority of twelve in the old Parliament, elected in May 2015. The prime minister was convinced, perhaps upon advice, that calling an election would enhance her majority. For the forthcoming Brexit negotiations, a large majority would provide her more room to manoeuvre, rather than be forced into a hard Brexit.

Opinion polls forecast a three-figure majority. The Labour Party under Jeremy Corbyn, a 1970s-type left radical was not seen as a serious threat. Indeed, within the Labour Party the dissatisfaction was so widespread that many were wishing for a decisive defeat which would clear the way for Corbyn's resignation and the reorientation of the party towards the centre.

In the course of an eight-week campaign, the Conservative lead over Labour narrowed as did the lead of May over Corbyn. One surprise was the collapse of third parties. Unlike what was happening elsewhere, the two established parties were commanding up to three-fourths of the total vote in the polls, a situation not seen for forty years. UKIP, an outsider party which had been successful in the referendum on the EU, lost most of its seats in local municipal elections when results came out in May 2017. It got no seats in the general election. The Liberal Democrats, who were the only group openly opposing Brexit and wanted to remain in the EU, were also not attracting much support in the polls.

On the day of the election, the central prediction was for a large double-digit majority for the Conservative Party. The exit polls told a starkly different story. They forecast a loss of twenty-four seats for the Tories, down to 308, and a rise of thirty seats for Labour to 261. This was the most unexpected result. But exit polls are usually accurate. The final figure was 318 for Conservatives and 262 for Labour. Together, they polled 83 per cent of the total votes—a record high figure. In Scotland, SNP shrunk from 56 out of 59 seats to just 35. The Conservatives won 12 seats, a figure not seen for forty years. The Liberal Democrats progressed from 8 to 12 seats, but no more.

The British results are thus unpredictable but, unlike in France, these reinforce the position of the two established parties. They confirm that the public is unhappy with normal politics in ways which we still do not understand. Labour ran on an old-fashioned left agenda and gained votes, while the Conservative appeal for a strong and stable government was decisively rejected. Democracy has thus produced another surprise. Conventional wisdom told us that a leftward stance by Labour would lose votes, but the opposite happened. There are more women MPs (202) than ever before, and more black and minority ethnic MPs as well. While Brexit stands as the decision the UK needs to implement, the UK may approach it in a much more flexible fashion than Theresa May had promised.

The one remarkable thing was the large turnout of young voters. Once again, social media was powerful in recruiting young voters to be active, but it also helped the Labour Party's cause. This impels us to look at the new voters through new perspectives. Old fears and myths about the left and the right require re-examining. The future is unpredictable; the future is young.

ACRONYMS

AAP	Aam Aadmi Party
AfD	Alternative für Deutschland
AIIB	Asian Infrastructure Investment Bank
BJP	Bharatiya Janata Party
BSP	Bahujan Samaj Party
CBS	Columbia Broadcasting System
CEO	Chief Executive Officer
CIA	Central Intelligence Agency
CIS	Commonwealth of Independent States
CPC	Communist Party of China
CPSU	Communist Party of the Soviet Union
ECB	European Central Bank
EEC	European Economic Community
EU	European Union
EVM	Electronic Voting Machine
FDI	Foreign Direct Investment

FTA	Free Trade Agreement
GATT	General Agreement on Tariffs and Trade
GDP	Gross Domestic Product
GST	Goods and Services Tax
HDI	Human Development Index
ICT	Information and Communication Technology
IMF	International Monetary Fund
INC	Indian National Congress
ISIS	Islamic State of Iraq and Syria
LO	Liberal Order
MITI	Ministry of Trade and Industry
MP	Member of Parliament
MSR	Maritime Silk Road
NAFTA	North American Free Trade Agreement
NAM	Non-Aligned Movement
NATO	North Atlantic Treaty Organization
NDA	National Democratic Alliance
NOI	Nation of Islam
NSG	Nuclear Suppliers Group
OBC	Other Backward Caste
OBOR	One Belt One Road
OPEC	Organization of Petroleum Exporting Countries
PAP	People's Action Party
PIIGS	Portugal, Italy, Ireland, Greece and Spain
PKI	Communist Party of Indonesia
PLA	People's Liberation Army
PPP	Purchasing Power Parity
PRC	People's Republic of China
PVV	Partij voor de Vrijheid (Party for Freedom)

QE	Quantitative Easing
RBI	Reserve Bank of India
RMHI	Real Median Household Income
RSS	Rashtriya Swayamsevak Sangh
RTA	Regional Trade Agreement
SDR	Standard Drawing Right
SNP	Scottish Nationalist Party
SP	Samajwadi Party
SREB	Silk Road Economic Belt
TARP	Troubled Assets Recovery Plan
UK	United Kingdom
UKIP	United Kingdom Independence Party
UN	United Nations
UNDP	United Nations Development Programme
UNSC	United Nations Security Council
UP	Uttar Pradesh
UPA	United Progressive Alliance
USA	United States of America
USSR	Union of Soviet Socialist Republics
VAT	Value Added Tax
WMD	Weapons of Mass Destruction
WTO	World Trade Organization

INDEX

Aam Aadmi Party (AAP), 93
Affordable Care Act, 103
Al Qaeda, 39–40, 42, 45, 47–48
Al-Aqsa mosque, 44
Al-Assad, Bashar, 47
Al-Baghdadi, Abu Bakr, 47
Ali, Muhammad, 38
Al-Zawahiri, Ayman, 42
American Declaration of
    Independence (1776), 1
American Revolution, 128
Angell, Norman, 123
Anglo Iranian Oil Company,
    15–16
Anglo-Saxon Protestant, 128
Anti-Americanism, 39
Anti-Corn Law agitation, 112,
    116

Anti-inflationary monetary policy,
    64
Anti-Muslim agenda, 96
Anti-trade rhetoric, 116–17
Appropriation Bill, 99
Artificial intelligence, 176–77
Asian crisis, 35–36, 151
Asian Infrastructure Investment
    Bank (AIIB), 151
Asian resurgence, 153

Ba'ath Party, 45
Bahujan Samaj Party (BSP), 94
Baldwin, Stanley, 155
Balfour Declaration, 44
Balkan Nightmare, 29–30
Bank of England, 5, 13, 35
Banking crisis, 2

Bannon, Steve, 68
Battle of Lepanto, 51
Battle of Waterloo, 1, 5
Bear Stearns, 57
Belgian Congo, 37
Belgium, Treaty of Rome, 8
Berlin Wall, fall of, 22, 26
Bharatiya Jana Sangh (Indian People's Union), 136
Bharatiya Janata Party (BJP), 70–75, 90, 92–96, 98, 105–06, 137, 157
Bhutto, Zulfiqar Ali, 39
Big Bang, 21
Black American, 12, 20, 25, 37–38, 46, 80, 129–31, 138
   admission of, 129
   civil rights movement, 38
   outmigration of, 130
   See also Slavery
Black economy, 89
Black Lives Matter movement, 25
Black money, 89–90, 94–95, *See also* Demonetization
BlackBerry, 34
Blair, Tony, 24, 41, 45–46
Bolshevik Revolution, 4, 42
Bonapartism, 174
Border-free movement, 26
Bretton Woods, 13, 151
Brexit, 64, 82, 86, 123, 125–26, 166–67
BRICS nations, 152
Britain, *See* United Kingdom

Brown, Gordon, 59, 86
Buckley Jr, William, 81
Buddhism, 155, 158
Bundesbank, 28
Burke, Edmund, 173
Bush, George W., 38, 45–46, 56, 161
Bush, Jeb, 85, 87

Cameron, David, 86
Capital in the Twenty-First Century, 82, 120
Capitalism, 8, 19–20, 23–24, 26, 30, 113, 148–50, 165, 175
Carlyle, Thomas, 51
Carter, Jimmy, 17, 81
Caste divisions, 160
Catholic Church, 52
Cattle trade, 96
Central Intelligence Agency (CIA), 22
Charlie Hebdo, 64
China
   border dispute with India, 158, 178
   Buddhism, 158
   capitalism, 148
   Cold War, 7
   control over Tibet, 159
   double-digit growth, 32
   economic growth, 56
   employment growth, 116
   export to Western markets, 119

foreign direct investment (FDI), 148
growth trajectory, 148
hostility to the Dalai Lama, 159
incursions by, 159–60
Japanese export-led model, 148
manufacturing sector growth, 32, 34, 116
miracle economy, 146
nuclear power, 147
One Belt One Road (OBOR), 152
Pakistan's allies, 178
Pancha Shila (*Panchsheel* Treaty), 159
peasants' revolution, 146
per capita income, 139
road in Aksai Chin, 159
largest economy, 32
Silk Road Economic Belt (SREB), 152
Silk Road recreating programme, 163
single-child policy, 154
sovereignty, 140
Tiananmen Square uprising, 148
transformation, 31–33
Chinese Exclusion Act, 130
Chinese People's Liberation Army (PLA), 7
Christian Anti-Semitism, 37, 51
Christian Democrats, 167
Churchill, Winston, 143
Civil rights legislation, 12, 80

Civil war, 5, 12, 37, 128–30
Clay, Cassius, 38
Clinton, Bill, 23, 55, 81
Clinton, Hillary, 3, 67–68, 76–77, 85, 88, 131
Cold War, 6–8, 10, 12, 16, 22, 29–30, 38, 40, 42, 136, 147, 178
  military war, 7
  mutual nuclear deterrence, 7
  reality of, 9
Columbia Broadcasting System (CBS), 169
Commodore Matthew Perry, 141
Commonwealth of Independent States (CIS), 22
Communist Party of China (CPC), 31
Communist Party of Indonesia (PKI), 10
Communist Party of the Soviet Union (CPSU), 22
Communist Revolution, 7, 10, 146, 159
Congress ideology, hegemony of, 137
Congress of Vienna, 5
Congressional hearings, 100
Conservative Party, 82
Constitution of India, 160
Conventional wisdom, 83–87, 94
Cow protection vigilante groups, 96
Crimean War, 43

Cronkite, Walter, 169
Customs unions, 115
Cybersecurity, 172
Czar Alexander II, 53

Darnton, Robert, 67
Darwin, Charles, 52
Datta, Narendranath, *See* Vivekananda
Davos (Switzerland), 34, 114
De Klerk, F.W., 23
Debt-to-GDP ratio, 28
Deindustrialization, 20, 78
 of Western economies, 78
Democratic Republican Party, 145
Demonetization, 89, 92–95, 98, *See also* Modi, Narendra
Deregulated financial markets, 24, 81
Deregulation of financial markets, 21, *See also* Big Bang
Dialectics, 26, 54, 127
Dollar convertibility, 12
Domestic violence, 25
Dotcom boom, 55
Downs model, 87
Downs, Anthony, 84
Duterte, Rodrigo, 2
Dutt, Barkha, 72

East European economies, liberation of, 24
East Germany, uprisings in the, 10

East India Company, 133, 140–41, 155
 Bengal Presidency, 155
Economic Nationalism, prizes and pitfalls, 110–15
Economic progress, advantages of, 64
Economic revolution, 112
An Economic Theory of Democracy, 84
Electronic voting machines (EVMs), 108, 172
Emergency, 137, 176, *See also* Gandhi, Indira
The End of History and the Last Man, 165
England, *See* United Kingdom
English Bloodless Revolution (1688), 1
Euro, 28, 61, 151
European Central Bank (ECB), 28
European Christianity, 168
European Commission, 27
European Economic Community (EEC), 8, 21, 26, 115
European monetary system, 27
European Whites, 129
Eurozone,
 crisis, 61, 87
 Greece bailout, 62–63
 member's responsibility for its own debt, 62
 setting up of, 61
 unemployment, 63

Excessive money creation, 55
Exchange rates, 12–13, 27, 29, 61, 122

Fabian socialist economic policies, 32
Fake news, 103, 138, 170
Fall of Bastille (1789), 1
Fascism, Rise of, 5, 143
Fascist movement, 104
Federal People's Republic of Yugoslavia, 29
Federal Reserve System, 5, 35
Feminism, 25
Feudal restrictions, 31
Financial orthodoxy, 167
Financial repression, 149
Financial revolution, 174
First World War, 4–5, 29, 42–43, 58, 122, 127, 134, 142, 153, 178
First-mover advantage, 117
France
  burkini ban, 49
  Cold War, 7
  two-party political set-up, 2
Free competition, 111
Free Trade, 4, 24, 112–15, 117, 122
Free Trade Agreements (FTAs), 115
French Revolution (1815), 1
Friedman, Milton, 19, 59
Friedrich List, 115

Fukuyama, Francis, 24, 41, 165

G20 meeting, 59
Galbraith, John Kenneth, 83
Gandhi, Indira, 136–37
Gandhi, Mahatma, 44, 134, 156
Gandhi, Rahul, 73, 91
Gandhi, Rajiv, 160
Garibi Hatao, 86
Gender identity, 25
General Agreement on Tariffs and Trade (GATT), 121, 150
German Federal Republic, 28
German
  hyperinflation economy, 28
  ban of niqab, 49–50
  Nazism in, 5
  reunification of, 22
  strong currency, 61
  two-party political set-up, 2
Glass–Steagall Act, 24
Global financial system, 5, 54
Global Gujarat Summit, 92
Global Village, 33–35
Globalist, 70
Globalization, 4, 78, 115, 117–19, 122–23
Gold–dollar link, abandonment of, 27, 54
Goldman Sachs, 100
Goldwater–Reagan–Bush party, 77
Goods and Services Tax (GST) Act, 98
Gorsuch, Judge Neil, 102

Goswami, Arnab, 72
Great Britain, *See* United Kingdom
Great Depression, 5, 58–59, 113, 120–21, 143
The Great Illusion, 123
Great Leap Forward, 147
Great Moderation, 34, 79
Great Recession, 58
Greece
   crisis, 62–63
   public spending cuts, 63
   two-party political set-up, 2
Gross Domestic Product (GDP), 16
Guerrilla army, 41
Gujarat riot, 70

Habsburg Empire, 42
Haj pilgrimage, financial help for Muslims, 137
Happiness Index, 33
Hayden, Carla, 67
Hayek, Friedrich, 19
Healthcare insurance, 103
Helplessness, 79–80
Hezbollah, 47
Hijab and niqab, 49
Hindu Mahasabha, 135–36
Hinduism, 74, 133, 155–56
Hippie generation, 76
Hiroshima and Nagasaki, 6
Hitler, 9, 104–05
Homosexuals, rights of, 50
Hotelling, Harold, 84

Human Development Index (HDI), 33
Hussein, Saddam, 18, 38, 45, 47

Illegal immigrants, 124
Immigration Act, 130
Imperial Preference, 113
Income inequality, 82, 118–19
India
   Aryan 'invasion' of, 156
   annual income growth rate, 33
   border dispute with China, 158, 161, 178
   Buddhism, 158
   cold war with Pakistan, 178
   effect of partition, 157
   exceptionalism, 153–55
      centre for Western multinationals, 154
      Five Year Plans, 153
      information and communication technology (ICT), 154
      mobile telephony revolution, 154
      population growth, 154
      strong economy with China, 153
   export to Western markets, 119
   fascination with Western liberalism, 163
   left-wing parties, 33
   Maoist Naxalites movement, 53
   market-friendly reforms, 32

multi-religious polity, 156
national question, 132–39
   Hindu–Muslim movement, 134
   partition, 136
   religious reform movements, 133–34
   revolt in 1857, 133
   Western education, 133
NSG sanctions, 161
Pancha Shila (Panchsheel Treaty), 159
per capita income, 139
The Indian Express, 72
Indian National Army, 143
Indian National Congress (INC), 134
Industrial Revolution, 7, 113, 140–41, 175
Inflation, 11, 13–14, 19, 21, 34–35, 55–56, 58, 78–79, 110, 116
Intercontinental ballistic missiles (ICBMs), 11
International Monetary Fund (IMF), 35–36, 62, 151
Interwar period, 123, 142
Intra-country inequality, 120
Iran–Iraq war, 18
Islamic Revolution, 38
Islamic State of Iraq and Syria (ISIS), 47–48, 125
Islamism, 41, 50, 168
   political urban guerrilla movement, 50
Islamist jihad, 37, 52–53, 168
Islamist terrorism, 168
Italy
   constitutional reform, 2
   fascism in, 5
   Treaty of Rome, 8
   two-party political set-up, 2

Jana Sangh, 136–37
Japan
   capita income, 144
   capitalism, 143
   defeated Russia in 1905, 141
   double-digit growth, 144
   economic achievement, 144
   export-led model, 148
   fascism, 143
   Great Depression, 143
   militarization, 142
   military past, 144
   model Asian country, 144
   modernization, 141–42
   Pearl Harbor attack, 143
   restoration of the Meiji Empire, 142
   rising curve for GDP, 150
   throwing the Western powers, 143
Jati identity, 108
Jerusalem, Muslim conquest of, 51
Jihadism, 166
Jinnah, 105
John Birch Society, 81

Johnson, Lyndon, 12, 69
Jones, Sir William, 155
JP Morgan Chase, 57
Judaeo-Christian tradition, 37, 51

Kennedy, John F., 4, 8–10, 12, 23, 128, 131, 169
Keynes, John Maynard, 7
Keynesian economics, 11, 32
Keynesian thinking, dominance of, 14
Khomeini, Ayatollah, 16–17, 38, 41, 166
   fatwas, 166
King, Martin Luther, 38
Kohl, Helmut, 19
Koran, 50
Korean War, 8, 40, 144–45
Kotnis, Dwarkanath, 158

Laden, Osama Bin, 39, 42, 45
Lama, Dalai, 159
Land Acquisition Act, 98
Lehman Brothers, 58
Liberal democracy, 18, 104–08, 150, 153, 160, 171
Liberal progressives, 167
Liberal trade regime, 123
Liberalism, 41, 122, 163
Life expectancy, 33
Luxembourg, Treaty of Rome, 8
Macartney, Viscount George, 140
Macron, Emmanuel, 3, 168
Mandela, Nelson, 23

Mann ki Baat (What Is on My Mind), 98, See also Modi, Narendra
Maoist guerrilla movement, 10
Maritime Silk Road (MSR), 152
Marshall Aid, 26
Marx, Karl, 174
Mayawati, 94
McCain, John, 67
McKinley, 53
Mcmahon Line, 158–59
Merkel, Angela, 65, 124
Militant jihadi movement, 50
Minh, Ho Chi, 12
Misogynists, 77
Modernization, 16, 141–42
Modi, Narendra, 70–74, 88, 155, 157, 161
   ascendancy, 138
   as chief minister, 71–72
   Jan Dhan (people's wealth), 94
   leadership quality, 98
   Make in India, 92
   Mann ki Baat, 98
   passionate about bringing money back, 90
   as racist/communalist, 74
   Sabka Saath, Sabka Vikas (All Together, Development for All), 92
   Swachh Bharat Abhiyan, 92
   toxic image in media, 74
   Twitter, 73
Monetary policy, 55, 59, 104, 120

Mossadegh, Mohammad, 16
Mughal dynasty, 14–15, 140
Muhammad, Elijah, 37–38
Muslim Brotherhood, 41
Muslim League, 135
Mussolini, 104
Nandy, Ashis, 72
Napoleon, 1, 111, 174
Nasser, Gamal Abdel, 29, 45
Nation of Islam (NOI), 37
National Association for the Advancement of the Colored People, 25
National Democratic Alliance (NDA), 71
National Liberation Front, 147
National Socialist German Workers Party, 104
The National System of Political Economy, 115
Nationalism, 3, 30, 64, 83, 109–10, 124–27, 129, 132, 166
   Alt-Right, 129
   aspect of, 123
   complexity on peripheries of Europe, 127
   as a dynamic force, 127
   homogeneity, 127
   politics of, 126–32
NATO, 48, 101
Nehru, Jawaharlal, 29, 97, 136, 136, 156–60
Netherlands
   Treaty of Rome, 8
   two-party political set-up, 2
New Development Bank, 152
New Statesman, 3
The New York Review of Books, 67
The New York Times, 169
Newton, Sir Isaac, 13
9/11, 40–41
Nixon, Richard, 13
Non-Aligned Movement (NAM), 29
Non-aligned nations, movement of, 8
Non-tariff barriers, 114
North American Free Trade Agreement (NAFTA), 78, 100, 109, 115, 131
North Atlantic Treaty Organization (NATO), 8
North Korea, 7, 24, 101, 147, 162–63, 178–79
   nuclear capability, 162
   Soviet-style economic model, 162
Nuclear Suppliers Group (NSG), 161

Obama, Barack, 46, 60, 129
Obama Presidency, 61, 80–81
Obama, Michelle, 67
Obamacare, reform of, 103
Oil Shock, 14, 58, 117, 120
Oil, price of, 13, 16
One Belt One Road (OBOR), 152
Online voting, 172

Open Market Operations, 59
Operation Desert Storm, 38
Opium war, 141
Organization of Petroleum Exporting Countries (OPEC), 13
Ottoman Empire, 29, 43–44, 51, 127

Padgaonkar, Dileep, 73, 85
Pahlavi Dynasty, 15, 17
Pahlavi, Mohammad Reza, 16
Pahlavi, Reza, 15
Pakistan, 39, 88, 97, 105, 136, 157, 160, 178–79
Pan-Arab movement, 45
Pancha Shila (Panchsheel Treaty), 159
Park Geun-hye, 2
Parliament of the World's Religion in Chicago, 74, See also Vivekananda
Pasha, Kemal, 44
Pax Britannica, 5
Pearl Harbor, 41, 143, See also Japan
Pen, Marine Le, 3, 168
People's Action Party (PAP), 146
People's Republic of China (PRC), See China
Perennial War on Terror, 42–48
Period of economic stability, See Great Moderation
Perot, Ross, 109

Piketty, Thomas, 82
Political ideology, homogenization of, 81
Pollsters, 67, 77, 85–86, 138
Populism, 104–09, See also Liberal democracy, 104–08
Populist revolt, 2
Portugal, trading, 111
Post-nationalist Union, 124
Powell, Colin, 67
Princip, Gavrilo, 29
Principles of Political Economy and Taxation, 111
Prophet Muhammad, 52
  sacrilegious cartoon of, 64
Protectionism, 115, 117–18, 121, 167
Protestant Church, 52
Purchasing Power Parity (PPP), 33
Putin, Vladimir, 3, 48

Qajar dynasty, 15
Quantitative Easing (QE), 60

Racial discrimination, 125
Racism, 2–3, 71, 125, 166
Racists, 77
Radical loony, 81
Ramakrishna Mission, 74
Rashtriya Swayamsevak Sangh (RSS), 73–75, 90, 105, 137
Reagan, Ronald, 17, 19, 21, 81
Real Median Household Income (RMHI), 82

Refugees, 47, 65, 123–24
   liberal attitude towards, 65
Regional identities, 107–08
Regional Trade Agreements
   (RTAs), 115
Religious education, 50
Renzi, Matteo, 2
Republican Party, 77, 81–82, 145
Resentment of America, 17
Reserve Bank of India (RBI) Act, 91
Reverend Ralph Abernathy, 38
Rhee, Syngman, 145
Ricardian principles, 113, 115
Ricardo, David, 110–11, 150
Rice, Condoleezza, 131
Right populism, 167
Rock, Northern, 57
Rockefeller, Nelson, 77
Roe, Sir Thomas, 140
Romanov Empire, 42, 142
Rouhani, Hassan, 18
Rushdie, Salman, 18
Russia, Asian crisis, 35
Russian Bolsheviks, 146
Rutte, Mark, 167

Sabka Saath, Sabka Vikas, 92, 106
Safavid dynasty, 14–15
Salafism, 168
Samajwadi Party (SP), 93
Sanders, Bernie, 87, 109
The Satanic Verses, 18
Schengen Treaty, 26
Scottish Enlightenment, 168
Scottish nationalism, 126
Scottish Nationalist Party (SNP), 126
Scottish Referendum on
   Independence, 86
SDR currencies, 151
Second World War, 6, 11–12,
   14–15, 29, 42, 44, 61, 113,
   127, 143, 153, 158
Sectarian dispute, 53
Sexual harassment, 25
Shah, Reza, 15
Sharif, Nawaz, 97
Shi'a clergy, 17
Shi'a Islam, 14
Silicon Valley, 21, 79, 118, 175
Singapore
   miracle economy, 146
   success of, 146
Singh, Manmohan, 85, 91, 161
Sino-Indian relationship, 162
Sino-Japanese War, 158
Slavery, 12, 129–31
   abolition of, 130
   birthmark of America, 131
Smartphones, 34, 170, 172, 174
Smith, Adam, 110, 150, 168
Smoot–Hawley tariffs, 121, *See also* Great Depression
Sole Superpower, 23–26
South Africa, 9, 23, 152
South Korea
   economy, 150

GDP, 145
  Japanese model version, 145
Soviet Union
  cold war, 7
  collapse of, 24, 30, 42
  mass causality in Second World War, 9
  nuclear missiles, 10
  planned economy, 5
Spain
  fascism in, 5
  two-party political set-up, 2
Speech-making, 171
Sri Lanka
  civil war, 53
  Tamil freedom fighters, 53
Stagflation, 14, 19, 58
  effect of, 19
Standard Drawing Right (SDR), 151, See also International Monetary Fund (IMF)
Statism, 19
Strauss, David, 52
Subprime mortgages, 56–57
Supply-side reforms, 21
Sykes–Picot agreement, 43
Syria, 43–45, 47–48, 100–01
Syrian war, 47–48, 65

Tagore, Rabindranath, 156
Taliban, 39, 45, 47
Tamil Tigers, See Sri Lanka
Tariff-free trade, 8, 26
Tax cuts, 21, 56, 79–80

Tea Party, 60, 81–82
  fiscal orthodoxy of, 82
Terrorism, 52–53
Thai currency, 35
Thatcher, Margaret, 19, 21, 24
Theocratic Democracy of Iran, 14–18
Third World economies, 117, 148
Tiananmen Square uprising, 148
Tilak, Bal Gangadhar, 156
The Times of India, 73, 85
Tito, Joseph Broz, 29
Tolerance, liberal policy of, 50
Transgression, punishment for, 64
Travel and tourism, 33
Treaty of Rome, 8, 26
Troubled Assets Recovery Plan (TARP), 57
Trump, Donald, 3, 20, 48, 66–78, 82–83, 85, 88, 96–104, 106, 109, 114, 118, 121–24, 126, 129–32, 138, 162, 164, 166–67, 170, 174, 178–79
  break rules of decorum and polite speech, 67
  detractors of, 97
  dislike of Muslims, 130
  economics of, 121
  everyone's attention, 20
  first hundred days, 98–104
  fiscally active, 103
  focus, 83
  foreign policy, 101
  inaugural address, 122, 131

master of the TV medium
new rules of politics, 75–83
power of judiciary, 99
prejudice against illegal
    Mexicans, 124
protectionism, 121
protectionist stance, 109
racist/communalist, 74
realism in policies, 100
revealed himself as unilateralist, 48
slogan, 131
solid achievements, 102
toxic image in media, 74
unexpected victory, 68, 76
victory margin, 68
vote bank, 78

UN resolution, 30, 38, 44, 46
Unemployment, 5, 14, 58–60, 63, 79, 93, 122, 174
United Kingdom (UK),
    Anti-Corn Law movement, 112
    choice of dress, 50
    cold war, 7
    industrial revolution, 140
    industrial superiority, 115
    international monetary system, 7
    joined European Union (EU), 2
    multiracial integration, 125
    nationalism in, 125
    race riots, 125
    radical political movement in, 112
    referendum to exit the EU, 2, 124
    religious schools, 50
    seaways for trade, 152
    Trade Union Conference, 41
    trading, 111
    wedded to free trade in grain, 113
United Kingdom Independence
    Party (UKIP), 63–64, 82, 124, 167–68
United Nations Development
    Programme (UNDP), 33
United Nations Security Council
    (UNSC), 6–7, 46
United Progressive Alliance (UPA), 71
Untouchability, 134, 160
United States of America (USA)
    bipartisan consensus, 61
    budget's double deficit, 56
    cold war, 7
    debt-to-GDP ratio, 60
    decline in manufacturing, 32, 116
    defeated in Vietnam by a guerrilla army, 53
    economic growth rate, 103
    Federal Reserve, 5
    gold stock, 13
    international monetary system, 7
    maritime security responsibility, 152
    shrinkage in employment, 116

trade deficits, 13
wars in Iraq and Afghanistan, 56
USSR, *See* Soviet Union

Value added tax (VAT), 27
Vietnam war, 12, 45, 76
Vivekananda, 74
Vote bank, 78, 107–08

Wahhabism, 40, 166, 168
Wall Street crash (1929), 5
War on Terror, 41–42
Weapons of mass destruction (WMD), 45
Welfare State, 12, 19–21, 23, 81, 177
Western hegemony, 14
Westernization, 16, 142
Westphalian Peace, 169
White Commonwealth, 126
White Revolution, 16
Women's movement for equality of social, 25

Workers' revolutionary movement, 146
World Bank, 33, 151
World Trade Center, 40
World Trade Organization (WTO), 24, 32, 109, 115, 121

Xenophobes, 77
Xenophobia, 2–3, 125
Xiaoping, Deng, 31

Yew, Lee Kuan, 146, 157
YouTube, 170
Yugoslav wars, 30
Yugoslavia, 29–30, 127

Zaibatsu, 145, 150
Zero sum game, 116
Zhang, Schwen (Hieu-en-Tsang), 158
Zia-ul-Haq, 39
Zionist movement, 44
Zoroastrianism, 14